KU-542-505

INTO BATTLE

Arthur Wallis

INTO BATTLE

*A Manual of
the Christian Life*

VICTORY PRESS

EASTBOURNE

ISBN 0 85476 189 6

Printed in Great Britain for
VICTORY PRESS (Evangelical Publishers Ltd)
Lottbridge Drove, Eastbourne, Sussex BN23 6NT
by Richard Clay (The Chaucer Press) Ltd,
Bungay, Suffolk

CONTENTS

INTRODUCTION

MODERN warfare is horrifying. I know because I have seen it—in real life. Many young people today don't want to know. Talk of tanks and guns, blitzed cities and blasted homes, turns them off. I don't blame them. But we cannot live in a 'dream world' from which all thought of war has been excluded. We are dealing with an ugly but inescapable fact of human experience. 'Wars and rumours of wars' there have always been, and the Bible warns us that they will be with us to the end. The soldier is one member of society who is not likely to face redundancy.

Equally inescapable is the fact of spiritual warfare. A man turns his face towards Christ and hits a mountain of opposition. He presses through, but is often tempted to throw it all in. Prayer is often such hard going. Old temptations return with a new lease of life. It is such a battle to witness. What does it all mean? It is simply discovering what the Bible everywhere teaches, that the call of Christ is a call to arms. The Christian life means warfare. This is not to use a metaphor or a figure of speech but to state a literal fact. It is simply that the sphere, the weapons, and the foe, are all spiritual rather than material. In using the military analogy throughout this book I am not expressing any sympathy with the brutality of human warfare. I am simply taking my cue from the Bible. Much of Old Testament history is devoted to the wars of Israel, to teach us how to 'fight the good fight of faith'. In the New Testament the whole concept of Christ's kingdom coming to men is presented in terms of a military invasion. Jesus used a parable about two kings making war to emphasise the cost of discipleship. He also stated that He had not come to bring peace on earth but a sword. In the epistles there are several references to the Christian life as spiritual warfare, while the atmosphere of the battlefield seems to pervade the book of Revelation which looks forward to the final triumph.

There have always been those who wanted the blessings of the Christian life without the battles, who 'say to the seers . . . "Speak to us smooth things".' When God brought Israel out of Egypt to lead them into the promised land, He 'did not lead them by way of the land of the Philistines, although that was near; for God said, "Lest the people repent when they see war, and return to Egypt".' In the end they spent the rest of their days wandering in the wilderness. Many are wandering in a spiritual wilderness today for the same reason. There is no room in Christ's army for those who want to play at Christianity, seeking the thrills and the frills, but shirking the cut and thrust of battle.

The mention of military life conjures up in many

minds such ideas as discipline, hardship, suffering, and other nasty words. But these inevitably have their counterpart in spiritual experience. If these soldierly qualities had been lacking in those first disciples, Christianity would never have got off the ground. The lack of them today is one reason why so much of our Christianity is anaemic, when it ought to be robust and strong.

This book is a battle manual of the Christian life. Here the would-be-soldier of Christ is first shown how to enlist, and then led on to the subsequent steps of faith and obedience essential for spiritual warfare. Most of the practical aspects of the Christian life have been covered. It answers such questions as, 'How can I become a committed Christian?' and 'If I become one, what will this involve?' Others who are already committed, and eager to be out where the action is, will find here much that will help to instruct and equip them for battle.

Today young people are being drawn to Christ in ever increasing numbers. I have written especially with them in mind. The conflict is becoming fiercer and the issues more sharply defined as the end of the age draws near. I rejoice that this hour of challenge is producing so many soldiers of Christ as dedicated and fearless as any who have gone before. To them, with whom lies the hope of tomorrow, I dedicate this book. May the Lord teach their hands to war and their fingers to fight.

I am deeply indebted to Denis Clark and David

Lillie who went through the manuscript with great care and whose suggestions have been most valuable. Also to Loren Cunningham of Youth With A Mission who helped to give me the American slant, and Major Mike Stevens who vetted it from the military aspect.

Those who wish to use this book as a basis of study would do well to read it straight through first, and then go over it a second time, carefully examining the Scripture references that are given at the close of each chapter. Unless otherwise indicated Old Testament quotations are taken from the REVISED STANDARD VERSION (RSV) and the New Testament from TODAY'S ENGLISH VERSION (TEV), otherwise known as GOOD NEWS FOR MODERN MAN. Both are available in cheap paperback editions. Where the AUTHORIZED (KING JAMES) VERSION, has been quoted this is also indicated after the reference (AV). Any matter in square brackets is mine.

ARTHUR WALLIS

INTO BATTLE

ON WHOSE SIDE?

WE live in a world at war. If it isn't 'hot war' it's 'cold war'. There is mounting tension between different nations and ideologies, between East and West, between Capital and Labour, between Black and White. Our homes are no refuge, for even there, so often, there is strife between husband and wife, between parents and children. People search in vain for a way out. Said an army instructor to a cadet, 'Your platoon is almost surrounded, you have lost several men, and you are running out of ammunition. As platoon commander what steps would you take?' 'Long ones, Sir,' was the reply. But man cannot take long steps to escape from his dilemma. He is like a hunted animal with nowhere to hide.

It is one thing to recognise the symptoms, quite another to diagnose the complaint and prescribe the cure. The fact is, man is at war with man because man is at war with God. Behind the human battle there is a spiritual battle. It is the age-long fight between light and darkness, between good and evil, between God and Satan. We are caught up in it willy-nilly. Neutrality is quite impossible.[1] It all began before man appeared on the scene, and will continue until

God's last enemy has been destroyed.[2] If you believe that God is God you cannot doubt who will win. To fight for the wrong cause is not only to lose, but because of the stakes, to lose for ever.[3] So the vital question is, On whose side are you?

Let us trace the river back to its source. In the beginning God made man after His likeness, to obey His laws and to find fulfilment in the enjoyment of His friendship. For a very brief span earth experienced a real Utopia as man lived in harmony with his God, and so in harmony with both his environment and himself. God had created him a free agent because He wanted voluntary, not compulsory obedience—obedience that sprang from love and trust.

Then tragedy struck. Man rebelled, thinking he could pull off a better deal with God's arch-enemy. By believing Satan's lie instead of God's truth he put himself in the enemy camp. The tragic results of his decision are not only all around us, they are within us.[4] Ever since, mankind has been suffering from an hereditary disease called sin. In infancy he has to be taught how to walk and talk, but needs no instruction in how to lie, cheat, and lose his temper.[5] Sin comes as natural as breathing. He seems to have a built-in bias against the will of God, and in favour of pleasing himself. 'All we like sheep have gone astray; we have turned every one to his own way.'[6] This is sin in its essence, turning to our own way instead of to God's.

By living our lives without reference to God we

have played into Satan's hands and put ourselves under his authority. Most people are completely ignorant of what the score is here. They find it hard to accept that the respectable, the moral, and even the religious are in the same boat as the avowed sinner. 'There is no difference at all,' the Bible says, 'all men have sinned and are far away from God's saving presence.'[7]

It is here we have to grasp the nettle. To acknowledge that we are part of the problem is the first step in discovering the solution. Many who air their views on 'What's wrong with the world' have never faced up to this home truth. Some years ago there was a discussion on this theme in the correspondence columns of THE TIMES. The following letter from the well-known author brought the matter down to earth with a bump: 'Dear Sir, What's wrong with the world? I am! Yours faithfully, G. K. Chesterton.'

One of the greatest obstacles to man's salvation is the pride of his own heart that will not permit him to face up to the facts. God says in effect, 'You have failed to measure up. You are weighed in the divine balances and found wanting. You have put yourself in the enemy camp.' But man's response is one of argument, of excuse, of self-justification.[8] What has your attitude been?

Jesus emphasised in His teaching that only as a man humbled himself to acknowledge his need could he receive salvation. Addressing the Pharisees, a group that suffered from an overdose of self-righteousness, He said, 'People who are well do not need a doctor, but only those who are sick. I have not come to call the respectable people, but the outcasts.'[9] In other words, 'If you Pharisees want me to heal your souls, stop pretending you are spiritually well and join the sick queue with the rest.'

Are you now ready, if you have never done it before, to bow your head and humbly acknowledge, 'All that God says about me in the Bible is true. I have broken God's law times without number. I have failed to love God with all my heart, and to love my neighbour as myself. In refusing Christ's rule in my life I have made myself His enemy.[10] I fully deserve God's wrath. I cannot alter this situation by any self-effort. I can only plead for mercy.' If you are able sincerely to make such a confession there is good news to come.

[1] Mat. 12. 30   [2] 1 Cor. 15. 24–26   [3] Mat. 13. 40–42
[4] Rom. 5. 12   [5] Psa. 58. 3   [6] Isa. 53. 6   [7] Rom. 3. 22–23   [8] Luke 10. 29   [9] Mark 2. 17   [10] Luke 19. 27

2

THE RESCUE OPERATION

FED by science fiction and reports of 'flying saucers', many have seriously wondered if the earth would one day be invaded by 'beings' from outer space. The Bible is the record of an invasion that was launched from heaven to rescue earth-dwellers from the clutches of a ruthless enemy, and to restore the kingdom of earth to its rightful Ruler.

You may recall the story drama of a famous French climber who was marooned for days on a narrow shelf of rock high up in the Alps. The temperature was sub-zero. Beside him was the dead body of his climbing companion. With a blizzard raging the prospects of a rescue looked bleak. Then, when the climber had reached the limits of human endurance, a helicopter appeared overhead, and the man was winched to safety. Weeping, he told his rescuers, 'I had given up all hope.'

The Bible is the record of a far greater rescue operation. It tells of God's intervention to save man from a predicament of his own making. He, too, was helpless and hopeless, and what was worse, he had made himself the enemy of the only One who could save him from his desperate plight. Consequently he had forfeited any claim to mercy or compassion. God had every reason to obliterate him or at least to leave him to his fate. Alternatively, He could have waited for him to come to terms. Instead He took the initiative and regardless of the personal cost, He launched a rescue operation to bring man back.

The price God had to pay to reclaim His rebel kingdom was the life of His Son. Here's how the Bible puts it: 'For when we were still helpless, Christ died for the wicked . . .' It is a difficult thing for someone to die for a righteous person. It may be that someone might dare to die for a good person. But God has shown us how much He loves us; it was while we were still sinners that Christ died for us! By His death we are now put right with God . . . We were God's enemies, but He made us His friends through the death of His Son.'[1]

If man's sin has alienated him from God, how is it that the death of Christ two thousand years ago is able to effect a reconciliation? We must first understand what God has to say about the consequences of sin. The truth that 'sin pays its wage—death'[2] is all too clearly seen in the history of man. Before Adam sinned he possessed a life that was not subject to death. In theory he could have lived for ever. But God put him to the test. There was one rule that he had to keep, and God warned him that the day he broke it he would die.[3] He did break it with the inevitable result.

Though man did not die physically there and then,

the moment he sinned death entered in a twofold way. First, he died spiritually; that is, he died in that part of his inner being that gave him contact with God. If you have ever stood at the open grave of someone you loved very dearly, you will know that death means separation. Spiritual death means separation from God, and if the situation is not recovered that separation becomes final. This is the meaning of hell, otherwise called 'the lake of fire' or 'the second death'.[4]

Then the same day Adam died spiritually he also began to die physically. The process of human decay set in, and in due course his body returned to the dust from which it was made. So, from the time of Adam there has been a reign of death over the creation, which means that man is cut off from his Creator, and his decaying body bears silent proof of the fact.

Unless we understand this truth concerning sin and death, we cannot appreciate the wonder and wisdom of God's rescue operation. This was the supreme purpose of Jesus coming down to live as a man among men.[5] The great climax was reached when Jesus gave Himself up to die on the cross. He was not an unwilling victim, for a way out was always open to Him had he chosen to take it.[6] Instead He trod with quiet determination the thorny path that led to the lonely hill top. He had said earlier, 'No one takes my life away from me. I give it up of My own free will.'[7]

When Jesus rose from the dead He explained to His bewildered disciples that His death by crucifixion had not been a ghastly mistake. Nor was it an heroic attempt to save a cause that was all but lost. It had been in the plan from the beginning, foretold by all the prophets.[8] Why was it necessary? Because death was the penalty for breaking God's law. If man had been left to face the music the race would have died eternally, banished for ever from the presence of God. Instead Christ had intervened, accepted responsibility for man's sin, and by dying Himself, had become 'the Saviour of the world'.[9]

Here then is the greatest drama in human history. The only Man on earth who never deserved to die willingly did so in order that men, who fully deserve to die, might not have to. The finest deeds of human heroism pale beside this supreme act of self-sacrifice. It is now possible for all who are the enemies of God because of their rebellion, to be reconciled to Him. You may now be rescued from the kingdom of darkness and death, and transferred to the Kingdom of His Son.[10] The way is wide open for you to quit Satan's service and enlist in the army of the Lord. But this will require a definite response on your part. If God is working in you He wants you to co-operate with Him.

[1] Rom. 5. 6–10   [2] Rom. 6. 23   [3] Gen. 2. 17   [4] Rev. 20. 14–15   [5] John 3. 13–17   [6] Mat. 26. 53   [7] John 10. 18   [8] Luke 24. 25–27; Acts 2. 23   [9] John 4. 42   [10] Col. 1. 13

3

TIME TO ENLIST

An important transaction must take place if a civilian is to become a soldier. He must *enlist*, and this will mean not only terminating his civilian employment but accepting a radical change in his whole way of life. The enlisting of the soldier of Christ is usually called 'conversion'. In this chapter I want to explain just what this transaction entails.

It is necessary to realise that there are two sides to the conversion experience. God has His part to play and we have ours. In the marriage ceremony there is usually an officiating minister who 'ties the knot', but the wedding pair are required to respond by affirming that their hearts and wills are in this union. Even so with conversion, it is God's work to free us from our old allegiance and to join us to Christ. But He requires our willing co-operation.

The Bible often speaks of this experience as a spiritual rebirth.[1] But birth is not brought about by the struggles of the baby but by the action of the mother. We do not become children of God by our own efforts, we must be 'born of the Spirit'.[2] There is a danger of so emphasising the personal response that we lose sight of the fact that it is God, by His

Holy Spirit, who convinces us of our need, enlightens us concerning the truth, and leads us to Christ.

On the other side of the fence there is a danger of some sitting back and waiting for God to take things into His own hands completely and convert them at a stroke. I once spoke to a man about his need of Christ. His defence was, 'Some day I will no doubt see the light', as though he had no further responsibility in the matter. No, we are required to seek the Lord with all our hearts.[3] We are commanded to turn away from our sins ('repent' is the old-fashioned word) and believe the Good News.[4] In this chapter I shall be explaining what this involves, but remember, salvation is God's work. If you are now seeking Christ, it is because God is drawing you.[5] You can only repent and believe because He is working in you.[6]

If you genuinely desire to enlist in the army of the Lord and become a soldier of Christ, then God requires of you a twofold response. First you must quit the service of Satan; that means *repent*. Then you must be joined to the Lord; that means *believe*. Repentance and faith are the two legs by which we enter God's kingdom.[7] People so often misunderstand these two words that I must say something about them.

'Repent' was a note sounded out by John the Baptist, by Christ Himself, and by His apostles. 'God commands all men everywhere to repent' (RSV), or 'turn away from their evil ways' (TEV). We cannot come into a personal relationship with Christ until we obey. Repentance is more than simply 'sorrow for sin'. If I were caught for speeding and given a heavy fine, I should certainly be very sorry, but that would not prove my repentance. I might just be sorry that I got caught! Repentance would mean sorrow for a good and wise law that I had broken, not just a resolve to keep a sharper look out for the speed cop!

Judas confessed with deep remorse, 'I have sinned by betraying an innocent man to death.'[9] Had there been true repentance in Judas's heart he would have experienced God's forgiveness, and that would have saved him from a suicide's death. You may remember that he flung those silver coins, the sordid price of his betrayal, on the temple floor. If, instead, he had flung himself at the feet of his offended God he could have found mercy.

To repent means to change one's mind. When a man repents he ceases to justify himself. Instead of excusing his sin he exposes it. Instead of siding with himself against God he sides with God against himself.[10] It is not that he is able himself to break the chains of sin—that is God's work. But God will only do this when a man's attitude towards his sin has changed.

Repentance always leads to *confession*. 'He who conceals his transgressions will not prosper, but he who *confesses* and forsakes them will obtain mercy.'[11] We must first confess to God, for all sin is primarily against Him.[12] If particular sins trouble us we should

23

name them. But where we have sinned against others we must confess to them too, and where necessary make restitution—that is, do all in our power to make good the damage done. For example, money or goods stolen must be restored with interest.[13]

True repentance will always produce a changed life. The verse just quoted requires us to *forsake* as well as confess our transgressions. In other words the change of mind (repentance) will result in a change of course. We have an example of this in a very simple parable of Jesus. A father told his two sons to go and work in his vineyard. One refused point-blank, but on his way home he had a change of heart. He turned round and headed for the vineyard.[14] That is repentance.

For a true conversion experience repentance must always be accompanied by faith, the other leg by which we enter the kingdom. It is faith in Christ that saves. Man finds a strong temptation to trust his own good deeds for acceptance with God instead of Christ alone. This boosts his ego. But God rejects and condemns outright all such pride of heart. Salvation, He tells us, is a gift, not a wage. This rules out all boasting. 'For it is by God's grace that you have been saved, through faith. It is not your own doing, but God's gift. There is nothing here to boast of, since it is not the result of your own efforts.'[15]

This faith that saves is much more than assent to mental facts about Jesus. I believe *about* Mao Tse Tung, but I don't believe *in* him. 'The demons also believe (about God)—and tremble with fear.'[16] but their faith doesn't save them. To believe *in* someone means to trust yourself to that person. If you are suffering from heart trouble and you really believe in a certain heart specialist you will be willing to put your case in his hands. Believing in Christ as Saviour means committing yourself to Him for salvation. Believing in Him as Lord means submitting to His control.

It is often at this point that someone who is earnestly seeking salvation is tempted to postpone the moment of decision. They presume that the matter is left to them, and that they can turn to Christ when they like. God has only one time for men to answer His call, and that is NOW. When we hear God speak and are conscious of His Spirit pleading with us, that is the time to respond. 'This is the hour to receive God's favour, today is the day to be saved.'[17] God makes no promises about tomorrow.

Has God been speaking to you through these pages? Do you sense that gentle pressure of the Holy Spirit within, urging you to turn to Christ now? If so, then you need to express this to God in a simple prayer. The Bible says, 'Everyone who calls on the name of the Lord will be saved.'[18] Find a quiet place. Kneel down, if this will help you to humble yourself before God. Then from your heart make confession to God and call on Christ to save you. It is not the phraseology that you use that counts, but the fact that your prayer, however stammering, really comes

25

from the heart, and is a real expression of faith, however weak. Do it now.

Did you call on Him? Did you sense that He heard your cry—and has done a work in your heart? In that case do not delay to confess Christ. The Bible tells us that salvation includes confessing with the mouth as well as believing with the heart. 'If you declare with your lips, "Jesus is Lord," and believe in your heart that God raised Him from the dead, you will be saved.'[19] Tell that one who is closest to you that Jesus is now your Saviour and Lord. Do not be ashamed of Him. It will certainly do something for your new-found faith, and bring a real release of joy. And who knows what it may do for the one to whom you witness?

[1] John 3. 3–7   [2] John 3. 8   [3] Jer. 29. 13   [4] Mark 1. 15; cf. Acts 17. 30   [5] John 6. 44   [6] Phil. 2. 13   [7] Acts 20. 21 RSV   [8] Acts 17. 30   [9] Mat. 27. 4   [10] Luke 18. 9–14 [11] Prov. 28. 13   [12] Psa. 51. 4   [13] Lev. 6. 5; Luke 19. 8 [14] Mat. 21. 28–29   [15] Eph. 2. 8–9   [16] Jam. 2. 19   [17] 2 Cor. 6. 2   [18] Rom. 10. 13   [19] Rom. 10. 9–10

4

PUT ON THE UNIFORM

ONE day early in the Second World War I walked into a recruiting office as a civilian and walked out as a soldier. I had enlisted—yet to all outward appearances I was still a civilian. The world outside knew nothing of what had taken place in that recruiting office. A few months later I was called to a training regiment and donned the King's uniform. Now I was a soldier for all to see.

Water baptism may be likened to the enlisted soldier putting on his uniform. The Bible expresses it this way: 'For as many of you as were baptised into Christ have *put on* Christ.'[1] To the man who has dedicated himself to becoming a soldier, the putting on of the uniform is a joyful and exhilarating moment. It does something for his morale, his bearing, his *esprit de corps*. All this and more, water baptism should be to the newly-enlisted soldier of Christ.[2] I once stood on a Californian beach and watched about 150 'Jesus people' being baptised in the sea. The 'love-joy' in their faces as they came out of the water and then embraced the leader who had baptised them was a sight I shall long remember.

Of course it is enlisting, not putting on the uniform, that makes a man a soldier. Just so it is faith in Christ, not baptism, that makes a man a Christian. Nevertheless, baptism is a significant step of obedience that brings its own blessing. It should never be viewed as a denominational issue. It does not signify adherence to any particular branch of the church. The New Testament teaches that a believer is baptised *into Christ*,[3] not into a particular church or denomination. This is a matter between you and the Lord.

How important is water baptism? It was the focal point in the ministry of John the Baptist, the Forerunner of Christ.[4] Jesus Himself was baptised in water,[5] and baptism had an important place in His ministry.[6] It was universally practised by the early church.[7]

Some of the most important teaching in the New Testament on the Christian life—how we may put to death the old nature and live in the new—is based on this rite of baptism.[8] God intends that as we submit to it there will be a release of faith enabling us to enter into all that baptism signifies. Very often, especially in heathen communities, when a person first professes faith in Christ, opposition and persecution do not break out until the convert takes the step of baptism. Certainly the devil takes baptism seriously.

'Baptise' is a Greek word that has been anglicised rather than translated into English. For this reason its basic meaning, to dip or immerse, has been obscured. New Testament baptism consisted of dipping the candidate in water. When our Lord was baptised He 'came up out of the water'.[9] Similarly, when Philip baptised the eunuch, they both 'went down into the water' and 'came up out of the water'.[10] This agrees with Paul's explanation of baptism as signifying a spiritual burial in the waters of death, followed by a spiritual resurrection.[8]

The command of Jesus to His followers to preach the gospel to the whole world has been called 'the marching orders of the Christian Church'. This great commission included a twofold command concerning baptism. He laid the onus first on the preacher, and then on his convert. The preacher is to make disciples from all nations, baptising them in the name of the Father, and of the Son, and of the Holy Spirit.[11] Those to whom he preaches are commanded to believe and be baptised for salvation.[12] At Pentecost when those who had heard Peter's message asked, 'What shall we do?' Peter replied, 'Repent and be baptised.'[7] Notice that baptism followed repentance and faith.

Baptism has a threefold significance. First it speaks of *purification*. In the hot dusty lands of the East the bathing of the body was an important part of daily hygiene. Sin in Scripture is often described as moral defilement, and its removal as a cleansing. This was the main feature of John's baptism, for it was accompanied by confession of sin.[13] The disciple Ananias exhorted the newly converted Saul of Tarsus, 'Rise

and be baptised, *and wash away your sins*, calling on
His name'.[14] So we see that in baptism we have an
outward washing, corresponding to the inner cleansing the Lord is performing in the heart and life of the
believer.

Second, baptism implies *confession*. It is an open
declaration for all to see that the one baptised has
truly enlisted in the service of Jesus Christ. This is
why, as I said earlier, it may be likened to putting on
the uniform. Baptism was never intended to be a
'hush-hush' affair. It was normally performed, as in
the case of our Lord, right out in the open in rivers
or city pools. Today, when a Christian is baptised,
whether indoors or out, he is declaring unashamedly,
'I have decided to follow Jesus—no turning back, no
turning back.' No wonder it is a joyous occasion.

Finally, baptism signifies *union*. It means that the
believer is united with Christ in His death and
resurrection. This great truth is unfolded by Paul in
Romans 6. 1–11. We have to think of the baptismal
pool as the grave and the believer's body as the
corpse. As Christ voluntarily yielded Himself up to
death, so by a voluntary act of faith we are united
with the Christ who was put to death.[15] As loving
hands then carried away that dead body and hid it
from sight in the rock-hewn tomb, so in the baptismal
waters we are symbolically 'buried with Him';[3] that
speaks of complete deliverance from the power of our
old life.[16] As on the third day Christ rose from the
dead, so we rise out of the water, expressing the

30

spiritual reality of our union with Him in resurrection, to 'walk in newness of life'.[17]

It is not necessary for the full significance of all this to be understood for a baptism to be valid in the sight of God. If the Roman believers to whom Paul addressed the epistle had fully understood the significance of their baptism, Paul would never have needed to give them the teaching of Chapter 6. In baptism we are primarily following Christ's example and obeying Christ's command. Once a person has truly turned to Christ and desires to obey this ordinance no one has the right to refuse his plea for baptism. If you are concerned about this matter go carefully through the chapter again looking up the scripture references. Ask the Lord to make His will clear to you, and then, 'Do whatever He tells you.'[18]

[1] Gal. 3. 27 RSV   [2] Acts 8. 39   [3] Rom. 6. 3   [4] Mark 1. 4–5   [5] Mark 1. 9   [6] John 4. 1   [7] Acts 2. 38, 41, etc.   [8] Rom. 6. 1–11   [9] Mark 1. 10   [10] Acts 8. 38–39   [11] Mat. 28. 19   [12] Mark 16. 16   [13] Mat. 3. 6   [14] Acts 22. 16 RSV   [15] Gal. 2. 20   [16] Rom. 6. 6   [17] Rom. 6. 4 RSV   [18] John 2. 5

5

EQUIPPED

THERE is another baptism the Christian soldier must experience, that is, if he is to be equipped to serve Christ effectively. Though in the New Testament it is closely associated with baptism in water, it is nevertheless quite distinct—the baptism in the Holy Spirit.[1] It is not an optional extra, but part and parcel of the full salvation procured for us.

It is important to understand that the Holy Spirit is not just a power or influence proceeding from God, but that He is just as much a Person as the Father or the Son. Notice how Scripture speaks of 'Him' and 'He' in relation to the Spirit, rather than 'it'.[2] When we first sensed our spiritual need it was the Holy Spirit who was at work in our hearts. Apart from His action we cannot be born into God's family [3] or enlist as a soldier of Christ. A man devoid of the Spirit is not a Christian at all.[4] It may help us to distinguish the work of the Holy Spirit from the work of Christ by saying: the Holy Spirit comes to do *in* and *through* us, all that Christ did *for* us by His saving work. It is by the Holy Spirit that God is at work in our lives.

Though it may happen at conversion, the baptism

in the Spirit is usually a subsequent and more powerful encounter with the Holy Spirit. It is when 'the power from above comes down *upon* you',[5] to quote Christ's own words. Notice that word 'upon'. It occurs constantly when the New Testament describes this experience. Even our Lord experienced the Spirit coming upon Him at the outset of His public ministry.[6] From that point the power of God was with Him in a way that startled and stumbled the worshippers in the synagogue of Nazareth, where He had been brought up.[7] His very last words to His followers before returning to heaven were to the effect that they would very soon experience the Holy Spirit coming upon them and empowering them to be His witnesses.[8] This was what happened at Pentecost.[9]

Years ago as I was reading in the Acts the history of the early church, I began to wonder what it was these first Christians possessed that I so sadly lacked. Certainly they were unsophisticated, almost naïve, by our modern standards. But what authority! what boldness! what joyous freedom! Our modern Christianity appeared drab by comparison. Later on I came to the conclusion that these people really knew the Holy Spirit, whereas so many of us only know about Him.

The Holy Spirit wants to possess us wholly. This is the meaning of being 'filled with the Holy Spirit'.[10] He wants to energise all our activity and to invade every realm of our spiritual being. Under His direction prayer becomes effectual and the Bible an open treasure store. There is a new release of our personalities in praise and worship. We begin to enjoy a lively sense of the presence and nearness of Christ. We are made aware of power at our disposal to witness and to serve Christ effectively. The Holy Spirit is the dynamic of Christianity.

The Acts of the Apostles records five instances of the Holy Spirit coming upon people.[11] In each case it was a distinct experience, and those on whom the Spirit came knew that something wonderful had happened. Generally they spoke with tongues, that is, languages that were new to them, which they did not even understand. Always there appears to have been some distinct manifestation of the Spirit's presence. From then on they seemed to be at home in the realm of the Spirit. Christianity to them was undoubtedly supernatural. Signs and wonders accompanied their preaching.[12] They healed the sick and cast out demons. In their churches they spoke in unknown tongues with interpretation. They prophesied and received revelations by the Spirit.[13]

Such were the weapons in the hands of these first Christian soldiers, and how effective they were to the pulling down of enemy strongholds! Of course not all were issued with the same weapons, but every soldier was equipped. 'Each one is given some proof of the Spirit's presence for the good of all.'[14] These weapons are still needed and still issued. Come to God, then, with open heart that He may equip *you* with all that you need to be an effective soldier of Christ.[15]

How is one to receive the baptism of the Spirit? The early church did not look upon it as a graduation diploma. Nor was it reserved for those who had attained a certain standard of knowledge, piety, or maturity. In every case following Pentecost it was upon new converts that the Spirit came. Therefore any believer may qualify. First there must be *an uncondemned heart*.[16] As for any other blessing we may seek from God, we must deal with all unconfessed sin. We must come before Him with a clear conscience. If a cloud has come between God and us since we first believed, then we must remove it by confession of that sin to God.

Second there must be a *thirsty heart*. 'Whosoever is thirsty should come to me and drink,'[17] said Jesus in this very connection. It is not that we covet someone else's experience, or wish to keep abreast with others in spiritual things. We must really *thirst for God* as a man marooned on a desert island would thirst for water. If you are not yet thirsty, ask God to show you why. The Holy Spirit is waiting to create that thirst as well as to satisfy it.

Then, there must be *an obedient heart* because 'The Holy Spirit . . . is God's gift to those who obey Him.'[18] Power is dangerous when placed in irresponsible hands. God's power is reserved for those who have submitted to His rule. The power is not given to enable us to carry out schemes of our own which we think may serve the interests of God's kingdom, but to do His will. The coming of the Spirit should mean that Jesus is Lord, for the Spirit comes to glorify Christ through the life that He possesses.

Finally, there must be *a believing heart*. The promise of the Spirit is received by faith.[19] The hands of faith that reached out to receive the Saviour's pardon must now reach out to receive the Spirit's power. Where people genuinely seek but do not receive, the cause is often unbelief. When God shows us unbelief in our hearts we need to confess it for the sin it is, seek full release from it, and ask God to give us the faith of a little child.

One thing more. God has put within His church the ministry of laying on of hands for the reception of the Spirit.[20] Of course, only the Lord Jesus can impart the Holy Spirit. He alone is the baptiser. But we see that He often uses the laying on of hands. Those who minister in this way, with the Lord's authority and direction, become spiritual 'power conductors' as they exercise faith on behalf of those who are seeking. You may be in touch with those who would be ready to pray for you in this way. But if not God will meet with you on your own. Do not rest until you have received the power of the Holy Spirit coming upon you. Without this you are ill-equipped for the battle.

[1] Mat. 3. 11 [2] John 14. 16–17 [3] John 3. 5–8 [4] Rom. 8. 9 [5] Luke 24. 49 [6] Luke 3. 21–22 [7] Mat. 13. 53–57

[8] Acts 1. 4, 5, 8   [9] Acts 2. 1–4   [10] Acts 4. 31   [11] Acts 2. 1–4; 8. 14–17; 9. 17; 10. 44–47; 19. 1–6   [12] Heb. 2. 3–4   [13] I Cor. 14. 26   [14] I Cor. 12. 7   [15] Heb. 13. 21 RSV   [16] I John 3. 21–22   [17] John 7. 37   [18] Acts 5. 32   [19] Gal. 3. 2, 14   [20] Acts 8. 17–18

6

ENEMY COUNTER-ATTACK

IT was during the Italian campaign in the Second World War. The Allies had advanced on a broad front dispossessing the enemy of the commanding position he had held. Immediately the order was given to consolidate, that is, to strengthen their hold on the newly occupied territory. As sure as night follows day, the enemy would be sure to stage a counter-attack. Troops are never more vulnerable than when they have just occupied but have not yet established their grip on new territory. Victory may be turned into defeat unless advance is followed by consolidation.

All this is so true in spiritual conflict. We are up against a wily foe, about whom I shall have more to say later. He knows when and where we are most vulnerable. The life of Christ has something to teach us here. There was a physical attempt on His life shortly after His birth. Herod was the agent but Satan was the instigator. Then there was a spiritual attack by Satan after His baptism and anointing with the Holy Spirit at the Jordan. Finally, in the garden of Gethsemane, facing the death of the cross, Satan had His last desperate fling. It is often so in

Christian experience. After we have been born into the family of God, after the Holy Spirit has come upon us, and then when we come to cross that 'last lone river', we are especially liable to the attacks of the Devil.

First a word or two about temptation in general. God permits it but does not promote it.[1] It is the Devil who is called 'the tempter'.[2] But there is still within us a tendency towards evil even though we now have new desires as God's children. The part played in temptation by this sinful tendency which Scripture calls 'the flesh', is well described by James: 'A person is tempted when he is drawn away and trapped by his own evil desire. Then his evil desire conceives and gives birth to sin.'[3]

Temptation is not sin. It only becomes sin when we yield to it. Jesus, the Scripture tells us, 'was tempted in every way that we are, but did not sin'.[4] Temptation has in fact a very important part to play in the development of our Christian character. A great athlete will subject his muscles to ever greater tests of endurance in order to reach his peak. A tree swept by the mighty wind will send its roots deeper into the soil. Just so God intends that the testings in the race of life shall serve to purify and develop our spiritual character to the full, and that the winds of temptation shall send the roots of our faith deeper into His love.

Though God does not cause temptation, He does control it. He 'tempers the wind to the shorn lamb'.

'Every temptation that comes your way is the kind that normally comes to people. For God keeps His promise, and He will not allow you to be tempted beyond your power to resist; but at the time you are tempted He will give you the strength to endure it, and so provide you with a way out.'[5] Job chapters 1 and 2 provide us with a very interesting back-stage view of temptation. It is seen as part of the age-long conflict between God and Satan, with man as the battle-ground. God put definite limitations on what Satan was allowed to do to Job, and did not permit him to over-step those bounds. It is so with us.

We are not simply the unfortunate victims of the malice of our arch-enemy, but the children of a Father who is all-loving, all-wise, and all-powerful. He is in complete control of the situation. He over-rules temptation for our good. He even promises a special reward to those who endure.[6] Little wonder James exhorts us to consider ourselves both fortunate and happy when we have to endure such trials.[7] Jesus also taught that persecution, which can be a very real temptation of the Devil, should cause us to 'dance for joy', so great would be our reward in heaven.[8]

There is one special counter-attack we need to watch. Being saved by Christ and being filled with the Spirit are experiences that bring very real joy. But feelings are variable, and that gives Satan his opportunity. We wake up with a splitting head, or the day seems to go all wrong. Our joy vanishes away. And then we are tempted to feel that perhaps this new experience, that seemed so real the night before, was just a passing emotion, and we are filled with doubt.

It is here we have to learn a very important lesson. Though God gave us emotions, and spiritual feelings of joy or peace are valuable accompaniments of our salvation, they are not the heart and soul of the matter. The Christian life is based, not on change-able feelings but on changeless facts. If my faith is ruled by my feelings it will fluctuate like the weather. If it holds fast to the promises of God,[9] not only will I keep on an even keel but my feelings will soon begin to behave, and the sunshine of God's love and joy will soon break through my overcast sky.

Someone has suggested that this kind of tempta-tion is like three men, Fact, Faith, and Feeling, walk-ing along the top of a wall. So long as Faith in the middle keeps his eye on Fact in front, Feeling tags along quite happily behind. But when he turns around to look at Feeling he loses his balance, falls off, dragging Feeling with him!

Now about doubting. Despite what some people seem to think, there is nothing pious about spiritual uncertainty, nor anything presumptuous about an assured faith. We are not required to live in uncert-ainty. When a person is asked, 'Are you a Christian?' and he can only reply, 'I hope so,' it is not a sign of humility, but may often be an indication that he is not resting on the true foundation. God wants us to

41

be sure. 'I write you this so that you may know that you have eternal life,'[10] wrote John to his little children in the faith.

So often Satan counter-attacks the new Christian with a fusillade of doubts. Our feelings and our reasonings are no defence. Faith must be our shield.[11] What does God's Word say? 'I will never turn away anyone who comes to Me.'[12] 'If you declare with your lips, "Jesus is Lord", and believe in your heart that God raised Him from the dead, you will be saved.'[13] 'To all who did receive Him, to those who have yielded Him their allegiance, He gave the right to become children of God.'[14] Did I come to Him? Did I receive Him and yield to Him? Did I confess Him? Did I then have the assurance of His response? Right then, let me rest on His word, whatever my feelings. God will never break His promises.

One thing more. This 'full assurance of faith'[15] is part of our heritage, but it depends on our giving continued allegiance to the Lord. If we rebel and take the bit between our teeth we must not be surprised to find that we lose the assurance of our relationship with God. The backslider will be troubled with doubts. The remedy is simple. To confess our sin, turn from going our own way, and put our hand afresh in His. Then we can lift up our heads to the world and declare with a ring of assurance, 'I know whom I have trusted, and I am sure that He is able to keep safe until that Day what He has entrusted to me.'[16] This is what the world is wanting. 'Give me the benefit of your convictions, if you have any,' wrote the German philosopher Goethe, 'Keep your doubts to yourself—I have enough of my own.'

[1] Jam. 1. 13   [2] Mat. 4. 3 RSV   [3] Jam. 1. 14–15
[4] Heb. 4. 15   [5] 1 Cor. 10. 13   [6] Jam. 1. 12   [7] Jam. 1.
2, 12   [8] Luke 6. 23   [9] Heb. 10. 23   [10] 1 John 5. 13
[11] Eph. 6. 16   [12] John 6. 37   [13] Rom. 10. 9   [14] John
1. 12 NEB   [15] Heb. 10. 22 RSV   [16] 2 Tim. 1. 12

7

DAILY RATIONS

THERE is more than a pinch of truth in the old saying, 'An army marches on its stomach'. Every commander knows that poor food means discontent, low morale, lack of strength and stamina. These in turn affect fighting efficiency.

Daily rations are no less important for the wellbeing of the Christian soldier. God has provided for us a wholesome and appetising diet in His Word, the Bible.[1] I trust that as you have read these few chapters your 'inner man' has been fed and strengthened. Though we are often nourished by spiritual food that others have gathered and placed before us—as is the the case with books we read or addresses we hear—it is even more important that we learn to fend for ourselves. This is essential if we are to become strong, stable, and effective soldiers.

The Bible claims to be God's word to men—the only holy book that makes such a bold claim. The proof is found within its pages, not in the arguments of those who would try to defend it. Spurgeon, a pulpit giant of the last century, said, 'I would no more think of defending the Bible than I would of defending a caged lion. The thing to do is to let it out!' Over the centuries it has been banned and burned, reviled and ridiculed, attacked by the critics and the sceptics. Still it stands unscathed, the most read, the most loved, indeed the most wonderful book in the world. Behind the great diversity of human authorship is the divine Author.[2] This alone could account for its amazing unity and harmony. Though it was men who spoke and wrote, they were men who were inspired by the Spirit of God.[3] Here then is the mind of God in print. The more acquainted we become with this book the more convinced we are that it is God's truth.[4]

One thing that the new Christian will notice: a new relationship with God brings a new relationship with His Word. How could you love the God of the Book, and have no affinity with the Book of your God? 'I'm fed up with this dry old novel,' said the daughter. 'Very well,' said the mother, 'Choose another, there are plenty more.' Imagine the mother's surprise when some months later she found her daughter avidly devouring the book she had thrown down in disgust. The secret? She had been introduced to the author and had fallen in love with him! That's why your attitude to the Bible changed so radically when you found Christ—a personal relationship with the Author.

Because of its unique nature we must handle this Book differently from other books. We do not read it as an intellectual exercise, nor even for its beautiful prose or its historic interest. Since the Spirit breathes through it, God speaks to us in its pages, and by this means our souls are fed. By it we are instructed, corrected, and encouraged.

How much nourishment we receive will largely depend upon our attitude as we approach the Bible. A good appetite is essential. Peter tells us that we are to desire it as newborn babes their mother's milk.[5] Beware of the periodical, the paperback, the TV programme that takes away your appetite for God's word. 'This Book will keep you from sin or sin will keep you from this Book.'[6] We must approach the Book with faith, expecting God to speak, and that we shall be nourished, strengthened, and blessed. We read of Israel, 'They heard the message but it did them no good, because when they heard it they did not receive it with faith.'[7]

Now for a few practical hints. *A regular time* for feeding our souls is just as important as regular meals for feeding our bodies. We need an hour when our minds are fresh, and when we shall be least liable to interruption. The early morning is the obvious choice. The discipline of getting up that much earlier is valuable, and our time with God prepares us spiritually for the day ahead. Why tune the fiddle when the band has shut down for the night?

If you do not already possess one, invest in *a well-bound Bible* with clear print. It is worth buying the best. What version? Even if your mind is already steeped in the King James English of the Authorised Version, why not consider the advantages of thinking

God's thoughts in twentieth-century English? It helps when it comes to communicating those thoughts to others. But some versions are so 'free' that they tend to be interpretations rather than translations. The Revised Standard Version and the new American Standard Bible strike a happy balance. But stick to one version for regular use, keeping others for reference.

It was a bishop who gave me, one of a crowd of youngsters, the best tip I ever received on reading the Bible for greatest profit. Here is his recipe:

1. Read it through
2. Think it over
3. Write it down
4. Pray it in
5. Live it out
6. Pass it on.

Read it through. But where to begin? Start with one of the four gospels. John is a favourite with new Christians, but it contains some deep teaching, so that others may find that Mark, the Gospel of action, is a better starting point. The books of the Bible were written as books, so read them through as books. Select each day a portion of suitable length, but don't bite off more than you can chew.

Think it over. This is where the chewing comes in. It is not enough to read, memorise, or even study the Scriptures. We must learn to *meditate* on them. Ask yourself, 'What is God wanting to teach me through this passage? How do these words apply to me?'

Joshua was one of God's great soldiers in Old Testament times. Joshua 1. 8 teaches us that meditation was one of the secrets of his success. Don't try to meditate in a hurry. It can't be done. Persevere, for it will take time to learn how to extract the nourishment from your spiritual food.

Write it down. Keep a notebook with your Bible and record the thoughts that come to you. 'Much reading maketh a full man. Much writing maketh an exact man. Much speaking maketh a ready man', wrote Francis Bacon. Writing down your thoughts will help to clarify and crystallise them, as well as imprinting them on your memory.

Pray it in. This is very important if we are to be 'doers of the word, and not hearers only'. Often we shall find that meditation is punctuated by prayer, or changes into prayer almost unconsciously. And it won't all be for ourselves, there will be intercession for others too.

Live it out. The Spirit of God may apply the most unlikely passages to your life. Who would have thought the book of Revelation contained much of practical application to us today? Yet we read in the first paragraph, 'Happy are those who . . . obey what is written in this book!' [8] This, of course, is true of the whole Bible. The blessing of reading is fulfilled in obeying.

Pass it on. This is how we share Christ with others, and so increase the blessing and the joy. A blessing shared is a blessing doubled, just as a burden shared is a burden halved. Don't be selfish, share your rations with others!

Jehoiachin, king of Judah, had been exiled in Babylon. One day his royal captor freed him, just as you and I have been freed. Then we read, 'And every day of his life he dined regularly at the king's table.'[9] This is our high privilege. Let us not neglect it.

---

[1] Jer. 15. 16   [2] 2 Tim. 3. 16   [3] 2 Pet. 1. 20–21   [4] John 17. 17   [5] 1 Pet. 2. 2.   [6] cf. Psa. 119. 11   [7] Heb. 4. 2 [8] Rev. 1. 3   [9] 2 Kings 25. 29

8

LINES OF COMMUNICATION (1)

DURING the fighting in North Africa in the Second World War, the battle swayed to and fro across the desert, with neither army able to clinch the victory. The reason? The problem of maintaining a fighting force that had swept a hundred miles or more beyond its supply base. Lines of communication are lines of supply, and when these are severed or stretched beyond breaking point the finest army will grind to a halt.

Prayer is our life-line in the spiritual battle. By this means we communicate with heaven and bring down spiritual supplies vital for the conflict. Let our lines of communication become over-stretched by too much doing and too little praying, or cut by direct enemy action, and we are soon in serious trouble. So let's talk about this very important matter of prayer.

In the opening chapters we saw that man at first was living in harmony with God, but when sin came there was estrangement and separation. Through Christ's work on the cross we saw how communication with God was restored. In fact, we now have a closer relationship with God than Adam ever knew.

Of all the blessings of our salvation, none is greater than fellowship with God in prayer. It is as vital to us as breathing, and should be as natural.

The point was made in the previous chapter that our new relationship with God is the secret of a new love for His Word. Similarly a right relationship with God is the basis of prayer. When as a kid I had done wrong and knew that my father knew, I could not look him in the face or enjoy his companionship as before. I did not cease to be his child, but I did cease to enjoy his fellowship until I had said, 'Sorry, Dad.' It is so with God. Walking in the light, or having nothing between us and God, is the basis of fellowship;[1] and this in turn is the soil in which an effective prayer life will flourish. The Bible states quite bluntly that God will not listen to us if we harbour sin in our lives.[2]

Often prayer is made to seem so complicated, but basically it is nothing more than the child talking freely and naturally to his Father. No special building, ritual, posture or phraseology are needed. Don't get tied up trying to imitate the 'Thee' and 'Thou', 'willest' and 'wouldest', used by some Christians. It may be a comfort to know that in the Hebrew and Greek of the Bible there isn't any special 'reverent' form of address for the Almighty, different from that used to address one's fellow, and that goes for many modern languages. True, there must be reverence, but God looks for this in the heart and spirit of the one who prays rather than in his phraseology.

51

First of all we should see prayer, not so much as a duty or a discipline (though it is both of these), but as a delight. The God who made us for His pleasure and glory, who reconciled us to Himself through the death of His Son, craves our fellowship. Jesus, our heavenly Bridegroom, says to us, in the words of Solomon's love song: 'Let Me see your face, let Me hear your voice; for your voice is pleasant, your face is lovely'.[3] Does a girl drag her feet when she goes to meet her lover? Does she find conversation with him a bore? Not unless there is something seriously wrong with their relationship.

If at first you find it difficult to become aware of God's presence, speak out the words of the Psalmist, 'The Lord is near to *all* who call upon Him, to *all* who call upon Him in truth.'[4] Remind yourself of the promise, 'Come near to God and He will come near to you.'[5] Then, in the assurance that He is listening, open your heart to Him. Begin to praise and give thanks to Him, for this is how we are told to 'enter His gates'.[6] If you find this difficult let the psalmist help you. Turn, say, to Psalm 34 and address David's words to the Lord until you find the Holy Spirit giving you words of your own.

Jesus spoke much about *asking* prayer, which the Bible calls 'petition', 'supplication' or 'intercession'. On the night of His betrayal He said to His disciples, 'Until now you have not asked for anything in My name; ask and you will receive, so that your happiness may be complete.'[7] So He has given us the right to use His name in prayer, or as a lawyer would say, 'the power of attorney'. What a privilege! He wants us to experience not only the joy of doing this, but that joy completed as the answer is received.

No matter is too small and none too big to take to God in prayer. When you come across prayer promises in the course of your daily Bible reading, note them carefully, and start to use them in your praying. God loves to be reminded of His promises, and they serve as nothing else to strengthen our faith for the answer. No time or place is unsuitable for prayer. Travelling to work, waiting for an interview, wrestling with an exam paper, handling a tricky situation. In the crisis of difficulty or danger, of temptation or trial, prayer should be instinctive. When his Persian monarch suddenly asked Nehemiah a crucial question, he found time to flash a prayer to heaven before replying.[8] That shows he was well practised in the art.

It is not essential to shut your eyes when you pray. If you pray, as I constantly do, driving the car, it is rather important that you don't! Incidentally, there is nothing in Scripture about shutting one's eyes. If it helps you to concentrate your thoughts, fine. Jesus lifted up His eyes when He prayed, as though looking up to His Father in heaven, and being a Jew He probably lifted up His hands too. Anything is helpful that stimulates your faith to realise that you are actually addressing a God who is right *there*.

Jesus once said, 'Give to others, and God will give

to you.'[9] This is a principle with God and applies to prayer, as well as to what we do with our pounds and pence. Just as we can be selfish over our material possessions, so we can in our praying. The remedy is intercession. It is right at times to pray, 'Lord bless me,' but it is wrong if we are never reaching out to others in prayer. This is the meaning of intercession. Reach out beyond your family to that needy family down the road. Reach out beyond your church, its ministers and people, to other churches in town. As you give in prayer, God will give back to you, and you will discover that God uses a bigger shovel than you do!

'Doesn't the Bible say that if we want our prayers answered we must pray according to God's will?' That's right.[10] 'But how can I know if I am praying according to God's will?' That is a very important question, and it touches another side altogether of this matter of *lines of communication*. Communications are not all from the soldier to his Headquarters. What about from Headquarters to the soldier? We've said a lot about our talking to God. What about His speaking to us? That is the subject of the following chapter.

[1] I John 1. 6–9   [2] Isa. 59. 2   [3] Song of Sol. 2. 14 NEB
[4] Psa. 145. 18   [5] Jam. 4. 8   [6] Psa. 100. 4   [7] John 16. 24   [8] Neh. 2. 4–5   [9] Luke 6. 38   [10] I John 5. 14

9

LINES OF COMMUNICATION (2)

IMPORTANT as it is that the forward troops should be able to communicate with Headquarters, to report on the situation or call for supplies, it is equally important that intelligence reports and battle orders should be getting through from Headquarters to the men at the front. There are many believers who know how to call on the Lord for their needs, but are unskilled in the art of hearing God's voice and discerning His will. So they never become seasoned soldiers, and their usefulness is limited.

Referring to Himself as the Shepherd, Jesus said, 'My sheep listen to My voice . . . and they follow Me.'[1] Don't think that this ability to hear His voice is a faculty that only some outstanding believers have, or that requires years of experience. Jesus is saying that it is characteristic of His sheep to listen to His voice and so be led. If you are one of His sheep then the desire and ability to hear His voice is within you.

God has made us dependent on Him for everything. As the soldier should not move without orders, neither should we. Jeremiah reminds us, 'It is not in man who walks to direct His steps,'[2] and Solomon warns us, 'Do not rely on your own insight'[3] or human judgment. In addition to the directing of our steps that we usually call guidance, we stand in continual need of counsel, rebuke, warning, teaching, and encouragement. At the close of the last chapter we posed the question young Christians so often ask, 'How can I pray according to God's will?' It is often the case that we need to hear God speaking to us before we know how to speak to Him.

How do we hear God's voice? Firstly through His word. I am speaking of something more definite and specific than the general comfort and strengthening we should receive when we read the Scriptures or listen to them being explained. Often after preaching I shake hands with the people at the door. Many may thank me sincerely for the message, but when someone grips me tightly by the hand and says with glowing face, 'Something you said really touched my heart tonight,' I know God has truly spoken.

It may be the text for the day on the tear-off calendar. It may be a 'chance' remark dropped in conversation or said in a letter. The Holy Spirit causes it to register deep within, and we recognise it as the voice of the Shepherd.

The Bible also teaches us that when we love God and our lives are yielded to Him, He orders and overrules our affairs for good.[4] So it is not surprising to find that He sometimes speaks through our circumstances. He may say 'No' by shutting one door, 'Yes' by opening another. When things go wrong you can be sure that God is speaking.[5] It may be in a sickness, an accident, a disappointment, a defeat, or through some unanswered prayer of long standing. It is no help to brush the thing aside and press on as though nothing had happened. If we would only seek the Lord about it with purpose of heart we would get the message.

When it is merely a question of getting the green light or the red light on some proposed course of action, God will often guide you by putting His peace in your heart, or by taking that peace away. There are many situations in which 'the peace that Christ gives is to be the judge (of what is right or wrong) in your hearts'.[6]

When there is a particular issue in which you need the Lord's direction, pray about it, and then wait in silence to hear God speak. When we read 'the word of the Lord came to' this one or that in Bible times it was rarely they heard an audible voice. Usually it was the 'still small voice' deep within. How does this work? I believe it is the Holy Spirit, resident in the human spirit, speaking to the human mind the thoughts of God. This means that under the control of the Holy Spirit we begin to think God's thoughts after Him. 'But is there not a danger here that we are merely thinking our own thoughts or even hearing the whisper of Satan?' Of course, there is this danger. We are in a spiritual battle, and battles tend to be dangerous, and inevitably there are some casualties.

But spiritually this is only when God's safeguards are ignored.

The question we have to ask is not, 'Is it dangerous?' but 'Is it Scriptural?' If God spoke in this way to men in Bible times, nothing has happened to make it any more dangerous now than it was then. It is by this means that spiritual gifts like prophecy operate. Of course, all prophecy has to be weighed and judged.[7] In the same way you will need to weigh what you believe is the voice of God. And do not be offended that others will want to weigh too what you believe you have received before accepting it. We shall make mistakes, but if our hearts are humble and teachable God will use our mistakes to teach us much.

Now for a few principles that will help us to tune in and hear heaven's signals, loud and clear. Although our minds come into play, it is with our hearts that we need to be concerned. Listening in to God is a heart rather than a head matter. What follows is not a technique in four easy stages, but four principles that will condition our hearts to hear His voice.

First of all, *humility*. Pride lays us open to enemy interference. It will also make us liable to self-deception,[8] thinking our own thoughts and desires are God's. When a person is arrogant or fanatical, not open to reason or willing to submit to others, you may be sure that the pride of his heart has deceived him. 'Humble yourselves'[9] is an oft-repeated command of Scripture. It is something *we* are required to do.

Then *submission*. It is here the will has such an important part to play. We may seek the will of God sincerely without realising how our minds are still influenced by our selfish desires, preferences and ambitions. God cannot get through to us unless we are willing for His will, even if this runs counter to our human desires. Jesus was talking about His doctrine when He said, 'Whoever is willing to do what God wants will know . . .'[10] It is equally true in relation to knowing the will of God in general.

Then there must be *spiritual sensitivity*. As we practise 'tuning in' our spiritual receivers will become increasingly sensitive to heaven's transmissions. There are so many Christians who have never exercised themselves in this matter, and so have remained 'dull of hearing'.[11] But even those who seek God in this way need to beware of those influences that come from the world that may so easily dull our spiritual sensitivity.

Finally there is *patience*, easy to talk about but hard to learn. It is right to seek God for direction. It is right to wait silently on God to hear His voice. But beware of trying to force God to share His secrets before His time has come. There are situations in which God will speak at once, but others when He keeps us waiting. It may be that developing patience within us while we wait is as important as receiving the message when it comes.[12] Of one thing you may be sure, God *will* speak, and speak clearly, if you will seek Him with all your heart.

[1] John 10.27   [2] Jer. 10.23   [3] Prov. 3.5   [4] Rom. 8.28; Eph. 1.11   [5] Josh. 7. 7–11   [6] Col. 3. 15   [7] 1 Thes. 5. 20–21   [8] Obad. 3   [9] 1 Pet. 5. 6   [10] John 7. 17 [11] Heb. 5. 11 RSV   [12] Heb. 10. 36

10

POSTED TO A UNIT

IT is impossible for a soldier to be an individualist in the way that a civilian may be. He is compelled to work in close co-operation with others. Every fighting unit is a *team*. If we have had the impression thus far that the Christian life is a very individualistic matter, the New Testament teaching on the church will provide a needful corrective. The Lord's army certainly does not consist of a bunch of individuals all doing their own thing. He has planned that it shall consist of many units, or local churches.

In thinking God's thoughts about the church we may have to rid our minds of some popular misconceptions. To many the church is simply the sum total of the various denominations, each with its own particular organisation. But the New Testament has nothing to say about denominations. All that we find there is 'the church'!—and very little organisation. Others speak of the building where people meet for worship as 'the church'. But again, the New Testament never refers to a building in this way. In that first century there weren't any special buildings set apart for worship.

We must listen to the Head of the church Himself

to find the right answer. Christ only made two state-
ments about the church, but they contain the germ
of all that we need to know. When Peter had confessed, 'You are the Messiah, the Son of the living
God,' Jesus replied, 'You are a rock, Peter, and
on this rock foundation I will build My church.[1]'
This that Christ called 'My church' and which He
Himself promised to build, is what Bishop Ryle
called, 'the one true church'. Only those who are
able to confess from the heart who Jesus is, as Peter
did, are on this one foundation, living stones in this
spiritual temple. All true believers then, regardless of
colour, race, or tradition, comprise the church. It is
the worldwide community of God's own people.

Later Jesus was instructing His disciples on how to
deal with a sinning brother. If he will not listen to
you, nor to the one or two others you take along with
you, you are to 'tell the whole thing to the church'.[2]
Obviously Jesus couldn't have meant, Tell it to 'the
worldwide community of God's own people'! Here
then is a different concept of the church. He could
only have meant the local congregation. A few verses
later He described it in its simplest form as 'two or
three come together in My name'.[3] Again note, the
church is not viewed as an organisation, nor as a
building, but as a company of people. Where
believers meet together, even if it be in field or
forest, cave or catacomb, *there* is the church.

These are the two concepts of the church that
Jesus gave us, the worldwide community and the

local congregation. And these are the only concepts that we will find in the New Testament. It is very important, as we pick our way through the confused situation we call 'Christendom', to keep God's blueprint always before us. It is not enough for a man to enlist as a soldier. Sooner or later he must be posted to a unit. It is not enough that you commit yourself to Christ and so belong to the universal church; you need also to belong to a local congregation. This is implied throughout the New Testament. There is also the exhortation, 'Let us not give up the habit of meeting together, as some are doing.'[4] Christians who live in isolation or who wander from church to church are robbing God, robbing His people, and robbing themselves.

The local church should be the place for further spiritual training. As we fellowship with others the corners will be rubbed off and our spiritual lives developed. Paul talks much of the church as Christ's body. As we discover our place in 'the body' we shall begin to function as a hand or a foot, an eye or an ear. We shall also begin to appreciate our need of the other members. Those who can't get along with their fellow Christians, and become 'lone wolfers' are usually unstable and immature.

In the tabernacle of Moses we see a foreshadowing of the church. There were two sections: the Holy Place where the priests ministered, and the inner shrine or Holy of Holies, where God dwelt. In the Holy Place were the table with its special bread, the

altar of incense, and the golden lampstand.[5] These
teach us what should be the functions of the local
church.

The table speaks firstly of *food*. The local church
should be a place where the Bible is honoured as
God's word, and its truths faithfully taught Besides
our own Bible digging, we need the help of those
with greater experience whom God has equipped to
shepherd and feed the flock.[6] The first church at
Jerusalem devoted themselves to four things and the
first of these was 'the apostles' teaching'.[7]

The table also speaks of *fellowship*. When we invite
someone for a meal it is for fellowship, not just for
food. The local church should be the place where
we share our life in Christ with others. Of course,
this is impossible where there is no life. Unlit coals in
a grate don't make a fire. But once ignited, the coals
need to be kept together to ensure a good blaze.
This is a picture of fellowship—the second thing to
which those first Christians devoted themselves.[7]
Differences of background, temperament or tradition
are no problem when we begin to taste the new wine
of fellowship in the Spirit.

Then there was the altar of incense, with its
fragrant smoke curling upwards. This in Scripture is
a picture of *prayer and worship*.[8] The first call of the
Christian is not to be a worker, or a witness, but a
worshipper. This is our highest function. There
should be scope in the local church for each member
to participate in praise and worship as well as in

prayer.[9] As believers we are all priests unto God, and there should be liberty to exercise our priestly functions.[10] This includes using any spiritual gift that God has given us for the blessing of the rest. The early church certainly made good use of the altar, for we read that they devoted themselves to prayers.[7]

Finally, there was the seven-branched lampstand giving *light*. This speaks of *testimony*. The local church was never intended to be an inward looking group taken up with its own blessings, but a lighthouse in the darkness of this world. Christ told us that we were to be salt and light in the world.[11] He expects us to be involved, just as He was, in the spiritual and social needs of the men and women around us. Certainly there was nothing inward-looking about the Jerusalem church. So bright was their light that we read, 'And every day the Lord added to their group those who were being saved.'[12]

A soldier is posted to a unit. He is not free to chose one that takes his fancy. You will need to seek the will of God as to where you should make your spiritual home. You will be limited of course to what is available in your locality, and only rarely will you find anything that approximates to the New Testament ideal. At all events give the local church that you attend your loyal and whole-hearted support. Whether or not it is a denominational church, keep yourself free from a denominational spirit. You belong firstly to the body of Christ, that is the worldwide community of God's children, and then to *that* local congregation of believers. Scripture does not require you to belong to anything more. This will help you to maintain the unity of the Spirit with God's people everywhere.[13]

If before your conversion you were linked with a church where the Bible is not truly preached, and where there is no living fellowship, don't assume that you are to cut yourself off forthwith. God may still want you there, at least for a time, humbly to bear your testimony to Christ. The Christians in Jerusalem continued to worship in temple and synagogue, until they were thrown out![14] But *that* wasn't their church. The fellowship we have been talking about they found in the homes where the believers met together. And if your former place of worship is unable to meet your need of food, fellowship and an outlet for service, though you still maintain contact with it, you will need to find live fellowship elsewhere, even if you have to travel a distance.

When we look at the worldwide picture of the church we see that a wonderful thing is happening as a result of the visitation of the Spirit. Barriers are crumbling as God's people discover the truth of what they have so often sung 'We are not divided, all one body we.' The situation has been likened to a flock of ducks, all from the same family, yet separated in different pens. Their only contact is to quack at each other through the fence! Then the flood comes and the ducks become water-borne. Soon they are swimming over the tops of the submerged fences, overjoyed to discover that they are one after all.

Jesus made this prediction concerning His sheep, 'They will become one flock with one shepherd.'[15] Also in that great prayer just before the cross He asked the Father that all His people may be one, just as He was one with the Father.[16] God is remembering that prayer. It will yet be fully answered. Let us not hinder this by sectarianism, exclusivism, or by any other sectional interest. Instead, let this goal of true spiritual unity be as dear to our hearts as it is to His.

[1] Mat. 16. 16–18   [2] Mat. 18. 16–17   [3] Mat. 18. 20
[4] Heb. 10. 25   [5] Exod. 37. 10–28   [6] Acts 20. 28
[7] Acts 2. 42 RSV   [8] Rev. 8. 4   [9] 1 Cor. 14. 26   [10] 1 Pet. 2. 5   [11] Mat. 5. 13–14   [12] Acts 2. 47   [13] Eph. 4. 3
[14] Acts 2. 46; 3. 1   [15] John 10. 16   [16] John 17. 11, 21–23

11

AN IMPORTANT COMMAND

MUCH of a soldier's life is taken up with receiving commands and obeying them. As soon as God had saved His people out of Egypt He taught them that obedience was the price of His continued protection and blessing.[1] I am now going to speak about an important command that is closely connected with the teaching just given on the local church. It is the command to eat bread and drink wine in remembrance of Christ.

Baptism in water and the Communion are the two great ordinances of the church. An ordinance is a statute or decree, and these two were given by the Head of the church Himself. This ordinance is variously called the Communion, the Sacrament, the Eucharist, the Lord's Supper, or the Breaking of Bread. It was foreshadowed in the Old Testament by the Jewish Passover.

The homes of the Israelites in Egypt had been delivered from the destroying angel by each household killing a lamb and sprinkling its blood on the doorposts of each home. God had said, 'When I see the blood I will pass over you.' The lamb was then roasted and eaten. From then on the Passover was celebrated annually at God's command, 'as an ordinance for ever'.[2] It was on Passover night centuries later that Jesus, in the company of the Twelve, instituted this memorial Supper to remind them of their Master who was so very soon to become the true Passover lamb, shedding His blood for their salvation.

All that the New Testament tells us about this ordinance is confined to its institution as recorded in the first three Gospels,[3] two passages in the Acts,[4] and two in 1 Corinthians.[5] It is interesting to compare the two ordinances. Both point to the heart of the Christian faith, Christ's death on the cross and our union with Him. Baptism, however, is a rite of initiation, and so does not need to be repeated. The Communion on the other hand, like the Passover, was to be repeated again and again—'as often as you eat this bread and drink the cup.'[6]

When the Lord took the bread He said, 'This is My body.' When He took the cup He said, 'This is My blood.' We are not to understand by this that anything magical or mystical took place in the elements, any more than any change took place in His body when He said, 'I am the door' or 'I am the vine.' He was using symbolism, and referring to unseen spiritual realities. This is another feature of an ordinance, it is a kind of enacted parable that uses the outward material thing to signify what is inward and spiritual.

We must not assume that our Lord's words referred only to His death. He did not say, 'This do in remembrance of My death,' but 'in remembrance of Me.' He knew that when the time came for them to do it He would no longer be dead, but very much alive. The Supper speaks of the results of His death as well as the death itself. For example, the bread not only symbolises His physical body, but His spiritual body, of which we are all members.[7] The cup not only speaks of His blood shed for us, but of the resultant life which is now within that spiritual body, 'For the life of the flesh is in the blood.'[8]

Breaking bread is an act of *commemoration*. The emphasis on remembrance is very strong. In asking His disciples to do this Jesus is saying, 'I want this meal to remind you of Me, and of all that I did for you.' We tend to forget so quickly. When, as all too often happens, I have to leave home for a while, I like to take with me a photo of my wife. But when I return home I don't worry much about the photo. Why should I, when I have the real thing? The Bible tells us that we are only required to obey this command 'until the Lord comes'[6] referring to Christ's personal return. When we see Him face to face we shall no longer need this reminder.

Breaking bread is also an act of *confession*. Here again it is very similar to baptism. Paul reminds us, 'as often as you eat this bread and drink the cup, you proclaim the Lord's death.'[6] It is not uncommon for an unbeliever witnessing the Communion service to find Christ, and the believer to receive a fresh vision of the cross.

Finally, breaking of bread is an act of *communion*. Paul tells us that the bread and the cup are 'the communion' of the body and blood of Christ.[9] In the passover it was not enough for the Israelite to slay the lamb and sprinkle its blood on the doorway, the lamb had then to be eaten, roasted with fire. In instituting this memorial Supper Jesus did not say, 'Look at the bread and cup on the table, in remembrance of Me.' He told us to *eat* and to *drink*.

Earlier in His ministry Our Lord had said that those who ate His flesh and drank His blood had eternal life.[10] 'But,' someone will say, 'I thought it was receiving Christ by faith that gave us eternal life, not taking Communion.' True. But receiving Christ is but the first act of feeding on Christ. By this I mean, assimilating into one's spiritual being His life and virtue, just as eating food means receiving its strengthening and nourishment. This is but the beginning of a life of communion. And the Communion service is intended to stimulate us 'to feed on Him in our hearts by faith',[11] not just as we partake of the elements, but continually. That's why the service is so much more than a remembrance of His death.

It is worth noting that this simple yet beautiful ordinance was instituted by Jesus in a private home, on a weeknight, and in connection with a social meal. It is a pity that its simplicity has so often been obscured by ritual and tradition. How often should we break bread? Here again, man has made rules where the Holy Spirit has made none. After Pentecost it would seem that the Christians broke bread every day; later on probably less frequently. All that Jesus said was, 'As often as you eat . . . and drink'[6] leaving the frequency an open question. Circumstances, and the mutual desire to do this will vary from church to church. Scripture, however, says nothing about a special time or place or official leader being required before the ordinance may be kept.

Though there is much joy and blessing in obeying this command of Christ, a word of warning is needed. It is possible to partake of this Supper 'in an improper manner'.[12] This is liable to bring the Lord's judgment upon the person concerned. Because of serious division among the Corinthians and misbehaviour at the Lord's table, some in the church had been afflicted with weakness and sickness, and some had died. Carelessness here may expose Christ's soldier to enemy attack. Before partaking of the elements 'Everyone should examine himself'[13] to see that his conscience is without offence toward God and man. If things are not right it is much better to refrain from partaking until they are put right.

Jesus said, 'If you love Me you will obey My commandments.'[14] Let us see to it that we are found regularly at His table, with pure hearts overflowing with praise and gratitude. In this way we shall be

following in the steps of those first Christians who
'devoted themselves . . . to the breaking of bread'.[15]

[1] Exod. 15. 26   [2] Exod. 12. 14   [3] Mat. 26. 26–29; Mark
14. 22–25; Luke 22. 14–20   [4] Acts 2. 42, 46; 20. 7   [5] 1 Cor.
10. 16–17; 11. 20–34   [6] 1 Cor. 11. 26 RSV   [7] 1 Cor. 10.
17   [8] Lev. 17. 11   [9] 1 Cor. 10. 16–17 AV   [10] John 6.
53–54   [11] Communion Service, Book of Common Prayer
[12] 1 Cor. 11. 27   [13] 1 Cor. 11. 28   [14] John 14 . 15   [15] Acts
2. 42 RSV

KNOW YOUR ENEMY

An army will make use of all possible means to obtain information about the enemy and his tactics. The Christian soldier, however, has an infallible handbook that will tell him all that he needs to know. From the Bible we learn that our enemy is threefold—the world, the flesh, and the devil. The world is the *external* enemy, the flesh is the *internal* enemy, and the devil is the *infernal* enemy! By 'the world' is meant the anti-God system that dominates mankind. By 'the flesh' is meant our fallen nature with its sinful tendencies. By 'the devil' is meant one who is not only evil, but the originator of evil. Of course, these three are very closely related in their working, as we learn from Ephesians 2. 2–3. But in this chapter I shall be concentrating on our arch-enemy, the devil.

One result of becoming a child of God is that the invisible and spiritual world, that hardly existed for us before, becomes real. The unbeliever, on the other hand, is dominated in his thinking by the material world. But the unseen world does not simply consist of God and His angels, it includes a rebel kingdom, with someone called Satan as its ruler. This is not fancy but fact.

Is it not rather old-fashioned to believe in the existence of a personal devil? Very!—as old-fashioned as the Bible itself. It commences, 'In the beginning God'—without stopping to explain Him or prove His existence. In the same way the Book introduces Satan, a personality standing in opposition to God, without explaining his origin, though clues are scattered throughout the record.

I believe in the existence of a personal devil *because my reason tells me so*. You cannot have spiritual power without spiritual personality. That force of good in the world which transforms and ennobles, implies the existence of a spiritual Being who is good. Similarly, that force of evil in the world which corrupts and destroys, implies the existence of a spiritual being who is evil.

I believe in the existence of a personal devil *because my experience tells me so*. Who has not known a sudden and inexplicable urge to do wrong that passed off as it was resisted? Also in dealing with those who have opened their lives to occult powers, I have been made aware of a powerful evil presence that could not be explained in human terms.

I believe in the existence of a personal devil *because Jesus did*. He had good reason. At the outset of His public ministry He was tempted by the devil for forty days, ending with a face to face encounter.[1] It is here that the usual arguments against a personal devil break down. Jesus was alone in the wilderness, away from other human beings, so He could hardly have been tempted by the world. Nor had He a sinful nature, so He could not have been tempted from within. How then was He tempted, unless by some personality outside Himself?

I believe in the existence of a personal devil *because to deny this makes nonsense of almost all the references to him in the Bible*. If there is no devil then what is this spiritual conflict that runs through Scripture all about? Who are we fighting? Not our fellow human beings. The Bible says they have been blinded by Satan.[2] Perhaps that's why so many of them don't believe he exists! 'We are *not* fighting against human beings,' declares Paul, 'but against the wicked spiritual forces in the heavenly world'[3] under the leadership of the devil. When it comes to the invisible world it is safer to trust divine revelation than human reason.

As to Satan's origin, it appears that he was created by God with the rest of the angelic host. He was 'full of wisdom and perfect in beauty'. He was evidently blameless in His ways until he rebelled. Eminent among the angels of God, he wanted to be pre-eminent. Pride in his beauty, avarice, and a desire to usurp the position of God Himself, are the causes given for his downfall. He was ejected from heaven.[4] Jesus said He saw him fall like lightning.[6] A considerable number of the angelic host was involved in his rebellion and also cast out. These fallen angels are the hierarchy of evil against which we fight.[3] Beneath them again are the demon powers that strive to take possession of human beings. Satan is spoken of as the prince or ruler of demons.[5]

Satan, then, is a created and hence a finite being. He is *not* all-powerful, all-knowing, nor personally omnipresent, although his influence is felt everywhere since his evil agents encircle the globe. He is under God's authority and can only act with God's permission.[7] We have already seen in the case of Job how God may overrule Satan's work for our good. No doubt this is one reason why he is still around.

The names and titles of our enemy reveal his character. *Satan* means adversary. He sets himself in opposition to all that is of God. *Devil* means Accuser, accusing God's people before God day and night.[8] The story of Job is a perfect example of this. Then *Abaddon* and *Apollyon* mean destroyer.[9] He is dedicated to the destruction of God's work. Three descriptive names tell us more. Because of his cunning he is called the *serpent*.[8] In his ability to intimidate he is like a *roaring lion*[10] hunting for prey. Finally we see him as *the dragon*,[8] a ferocious winged monster, with supernatural powers. He is called the wicked one, the tempter, the thief, the liar, and the murderer. Surely the personification of all evil.

Three titles reveal his present position in relation to this world. Jesus called him *the ruler of this world*.[11] It was no empty boast when he offered Jesus all the kingdoms of the world if He would fall down and worship him. He is called *the prince or ruler of the power of the air*,[12] so that his sphere of operations is the heavens that envelop this earth. Lastly, he is *the god of this world*.[13] It has ever been his evil intention to seduce men to worship him instead of God. No wonder John says, 'the whole world is in the power of the evil one.'[14]

This battle between God and Satan is the conflict of history. The cross of Christ is 'the climax of history'.[15] It was there that Satan was decisively beaten. On the eve of that stupendous victory Jesus said, 'Now the ruler of this world will be overthrown.' And so he was. His authority was destroyed, and final victory guaranteed.[16] The cross is the only basis on which the soldier of Christ is able to resist Satan and stand victorious on the field of battle. Does it seem that our enemy, despite the victory of Christ, is still having immense success? The fact remains that the high court of heaven has passed sentence. His ultimate doom is assured. Meanwhile God gives him plenty of rope. But the day is coming when the sentence will be executed, and the devil and his angels will be cast into the lake of fire.[17] But for the moment he is a force to be reckoned with. In the next chapter I want to speak about his tactics.

[1] Mat. 4. 1–11   [2] 2 Cor. 4. 4   [3] Eph. 6. 11–12   [4] Isa. 14. 12–15; Ezek. 28. 11–17   [5] Mat. 12. 24   [6] Luke 10. 18   [7] Job 1 . 12; 2. 6   [8] Rev. 12. 9–10   [9] Rev. 9. 11   [10] 1 Pet. 5. 8   [11] John 12. 31; 14. 30; 16. 11   [12] Eph. 2 . 2 RSV   [13] 2 Cor. 4. 4   [14] 1 John 5. 19 RSV   [15] Heb . 9. 26 NEB   [16] Heb. 2. 14   [17] Rev. 20. 10

13

ENEMY TACTICS

THOUGH himself invisible, Satan has left his foot-prints on the sands of history for all discerning eyes to see. The subject is vast, so that we shall only deal here with the two great examples of his tactics in Scripture. These will help us to identify the tempter's trail. The rest the Holy Spirit will teach us through Scripture and experience.

Satan's first appearance in human history is re-corded in Genesis 3. 1–7. He came in the guise of a serpent to tempt our first parents, and we are told that he was 'more subtle' than any other of God's creatures. There are three instructive words in the New Testament that refer to this characteristic of Satan. It speaks of his '*plans*'[1] (designs RSV). He is a clever strategist with thousands of years of experience. He lays his plans carefully and pursues them with relentless determination. Then it speaks of his '*tricks*'[2] (wiles RSV). This warns us of his cunning, stealth, and power to deceive. It speaks too of his '*trap*'[3] (snare RSV), the method by which the un-wary are lured and taken.

When Satan tempted the first pair in the garden, he chose a flank attack rather than a frontal assault.

He attacked the man through the woman. Adam was not deceived by the serpent, but Eve was.[4] The serpent then used the woman to tempt the man. The enemy will often attack us indirectly through those who are closest to us, especially if the relationship is not wholly yielded to God.

Notice the subtlety of Satan's approach to the woman. 'Did God say, "You shall not eat of every tree of the garden?"' The answer was, 'No' for only the one tree had been forbidden. But the question was calculated to create doubt and confusion, the 'softening up' process before the main strike. Though Eve parried the thrust, it was followed by another that penetrated her defences. 'You will not die. For God knows that when you eat of it your eyes will be opened, and you will be like God, knowing good and evil.'

This was intended to blacken God's character, suggesting that God had lied to them in telling them they would die, and that His motive in doing so was to deny them what would be for their advancement. The woman was also being lured with the bait of self-interest. The fire of unholy ambition—to be like God—was kindling within her. This was how Satan himself had fallen, and now he is seeding that same rebellion in the woman's heart. Having undermined God's authority he is encouraging her to assert her own.

Eve began to contemplate the forbidden fruit. She saw it was 'good for food'. Temptation often comes through our bodily appetites. She saw it was 'a delight to the eyes'. Through eyegate—the word that is read or the picture that is seen—Satan is still capturing the minds of men. Finally, she was convinced that it was a tree 'to be desired to make one wise'. This was a temptation to pride. This wisdom was not the sort that comes down from heaven, but what is 'earthly, unspiritual, devilish'.[5] John might have been summarising this temptation in the garden when he said, 'For all that is in the world, the lust of the flesh and the lust of the eyes and the pride of life, is not of the Father but is of the world.'[6] So Eve took the forbidden fruit and shared it with her husband. Round One to Satan.

Four thousand years later Christ, 'the last Adam',[7] was also tempted to eat. This was not in Eden but in the wilderness. Nor had He a body well nourished by the produce of a garden, but one gripped by intense hunger after forty days of fasting. Where Adam fell Christ triumphed. Read the account in Matthew 4. 1–11.[8] 'If you are God's Son, order these stones to turn into bread.' No doubt our Lord was conscious of those supernatural powers, as yet unused, stirring within Him. Had they not been given to prove that He was truly the Son of God? Could He not now use them to vindicate Himself before the eyes of the unseen world, and at the same time to satisfy His intense but quite legitimate hunger?

But Jesus knew it was the Father's business to vindicate His Servant. The Spirit of God had led

Him into the desert where there was no food. He gladly accepted the situation, hunger and all, as part of heaven's plan. Those supernatural powers had been given Him, not to escape from the will of God, but to do the will of God. He would not use them at the suggestion of the devil, but only at the Father's direction.

'Man cannot live on bread alone, but on every word that God speaks.' How right were His priorities. The spiritual took precedence over the material, pleasing the Father over pleasing Himself. As He later expressed it, 'My food . . . is to obey the will of Him who sent Me.'[9] Satan had invited Him to vindicate Himself. Instead He had vindicated the will of God His Father.

Again the devil attacked. Taking Jesus to the Holy City he set Him on the highest point of the Temple and said, 'If you are God's Son throw yourself down to the ground,' backing up the point with a Scripture that promised angelic protection. Satan is good at quoting and misapplying scripture to suit his own ends. Now Jesus was being tempted to vindicate Himself before the eyes of men.

The Jews were mistakenly looking for one who would set them free from the Roman yoke. If He now made a supernatural descent into the midst of the temple worshippers, would they not acclaim Him as the Son of God? Would they not believe that the ancient prophecy of Malachi was being fulfilled: 'The Lord whom you seek will suddenly come to

His temple?'[10] What a dramatic commencement to His ministry!

Jesus perceived at once the evil that lay at the root of Satan's suggestion. To act in a way that would require God to intervene for His Son's protection would be to tempt providence, and again to act in independence of God. It is sinful to try to force God's hand. 'You must not put the Lord your God to the test,' quoted Jesus. To have flung Himself down would not have been an act of faith, but of presumption. It is wrong to wrest the initiative from God.

Finally, from a very high mountain the devil showed Jesus all the kingdoms of the world and their greatness. 'All this I will give you . . . if you kneel down and worship me.' Satan asserted that he had authority to make the offer,[11] and Jesus never questioned this. In fact He later referred to him as 'the ruler of this world'.[12]

Jesus knew that one day those kingdoms would be His, for the Father had promised Him this.[13] But now the rebel ruler was offering Him this on the cheap. No rejection, no suffering, no crucifixion. It was the crown without the cross, but on Satan's terms—'if you kneel down and worship me'—in other words, 'If you acknowledge me as God.' This is Satan's one passion, to be acclaimed as God. Jesus finally repulsed Satan by quoting, 'Worship the Lord your God and serve only Him.'

As with the first pair, Satan tempted Jesus to act

contrary to God's will for personal advantage. Jesus met each temptation as a man, wielded the sword of the Spirit which is God's word, and vanquished the enemy.

Remember Satan is a spirit and so his working is supernatural. Notice how he transported Christ to the pinnacle of the temple and to the high mountain, and then showed Him the world in the flash of a second. Because something is supernatural is no proof that it is of God. Satan tries to counterfeit everything that God does. That's why we are told to 'test the spirits'.[14] 'Even Satan can change himself to look like an angel of light!'[15]

The supernatural realm that Satan operates we call 'the occult'. It includes all forms of spiritism, magic (black or white), fortune telling, astrology, horoscopes, ouija etc. Steer completely clear of all these. Real powers are operating, but they are evil and plainly forbidden.[16] Other things like hypnotism, clairvoyance, colour therapy etc. may not necessarily be occult, but may very easily become so, and one is wise to leave them completely alone. If you have dabbled in any of these before you became a Christian, even in fun, it is important that you confess this to the Lord, and in Jesus' name claim deliverance from any 'brush off' which could affect spirit, mind, or body.

Finally, try not to see Satan any bigger or smaller than you see him in the Scripture. Some Christians seem to have a very big Satan and a very small Jesus.

This ends up in a bondage of fear. Others have so minimised his influence that they are blind to much of his activity, and so play into his hands. Just as every ship is built to float and every plane to fly, so every Christian has been created to overcome Satan and all his works.

[1] 2 Cor. 2. 11   [2] Eph. 6. 11   [3] 1 Tim. 3. 7; 2 Tim. 2. 26
[4] 1 Tim. 2. 14   [5] Jam. 3. 15 RSV   [6] 1 John 2. 16 RSV
[7] 1 Cor. 15. 45   [8] See also Luke 4. 1–13   [9] John 4. 34
[10] Mal. 3. 1   [11] Luke 4. 6   [12] John 12. 31   [13] Heb. 1. 2; Rev. 11. 15   [14] 1 John 4. 1 RSV   [15] 2. Cor. 11. 14
[16] Lev. 19. 26, 31; Deut. 18. 10–14; Acts 16. 16–19; 2 Thess. 2. 9–11

14

DEFENSIVE WARFARE

CONTINUOUS victory depends on learning the secrets of defensive warfare. God can never use us to attack the enemy's position until we have first learned to defend our own. What is our position? It is summed up in that little expression, 'in Christ'. By this is meant our union with Christ and all the blessing that results from that union. Look at the epistle to the Ephesians. In the first chapter we learn of our blessings in Christ in the heavenly world,[1] and in the last chapter of our battles.[2] The blessings are to fit us for the battles.

We have already seen something of our union with Christ in His death, burial, and resurrection, as signified by water baptism. Now we must see in Ephesians our union with Christ in His ascension.[3] The power at work in us is the very same as that which raised Christ from the dead, and seated Him at the Father's right hand. Every power in the universe is now beneath His feet,[4] and so beneath our feet too since we are in Him. This is the position of victory that Christ has won for us.

God has '*made* us sit with Him'.[5] We didn't climb

up there by our own efforts, He put us there. Read Ephesians 1. 16–2. 7 and ask God to show you how you can have your feet on terra firma and yet spiritually be seated with Christ in that heavenly realm. It is not enough to grasp it with the mind, you must believe it in your heart. The effect in your Christian life will be far-reaching. Instead of fighting *for* a position of victory you will be fighting *from* a position of victory. What a difference when we are looking down on the enemy, as Christ is, instead of looking up at him.

The warfare of Ephesians 6. 10–17 which we shall consider in this chapter is primarily a holding operation. The armour is all defensive; it is to enable you to 'stand up against . . . resist . . . hold your ground'.[6] In this battle it is the devil that has to do the attacking. For complete victory you have only to defend what Christ has won.

Before we don the armour Paul tells us, 'Build up your strength in union with the Lord.'[7] Try lifting a suit of armour and you will know what Paul is talking about! In himself the Christian is as weak spiritually as any other man. He must confess his weakness continually and by faith draw his strength from the Lord.

What then is the armour, viewed as a whole? Elsewhere we are told, 'Put on the Lord Jesus Christ.'[8] In a word, the armour is Christ. This accords with Old Testament teaching where the Lord is ever His people's defence. 'The Lord is my rock, and my fortress, and my deliverer . . . in whom I take refuge, my shield . . . my stronghold.' [9] Considered in detail, the armour is the varied protection we have in Christ. By faith we must take it piece by piece. Twice Paul instructs us to use 'the *whole* armour of God'.[10] The devil is no fool. He will attack where we are unprotected.

In studying the armour, I shall quote from the RSV. The first three are basic pieces to be put on *in preparation* for the battle. Notice the past tense: 'Stand therefore, *having girded* . . . *having put on* . . . *having shod*.' Then the tense changes: '*taking* the shield . . . *take* the helmet . . . and the sword.' These may be seized and used in the moment of battle. Another writer has put it very aptly: 'A soldier is sitting in his tent and he is waiting for the battle call. He has on his belt, his breastplate and his boots; and suddenly the bugle blows. He picks up his shield, he puts on his helmet, he grasps his sword—and he is ready for battle!'[11]

The girdle is rather different from the belt of the modern soldier. The oriental wore a long robe. Girding the loins signifies gathering it at the waist with a girdle. It was loosened for rest and tightened for action. If a soldier was not girded he would certainly be impeded, and most probably tripped, in the battle. In naval language it means 'clearing the decks for action'.

To express this in practical terms, we must deal with every encumbrance that would hinder us in the fight. In another passage a similar thought is expressed when the Christian life is likened to a marathon: 'Let us rid ourselves, then, of everything that gets in the way, and the sin which holds on to us so tightly, and let us run with determination the race.'[12] 'Everything that gets in the way' may include things which are not in themselves sinful. 'All things are lawful for me,' says Paul, 'but not all things are helpful.'[13] It may not be against the rules for an Olympic miler to wear a heavy overcoat, but it certainly wouldn't be helpful! There may be habits, ambitions, pastimes, attitudes, and so on, that may be alright for the Christian 'civilian' (a contradiction in terms) but not for the Christian soldier.

We are to gird our loins with *truth*. Jesus said 'the truth will make you free;' and again, 'the Son makes you free.'[14] *He* then is the truth. *He* is the girdle. Don't wait for the dust and din of battle before you deal with those hindering things. Come in faith to the Son and let Him free you now.

Next is *the breastplate of righteousness*. The breast suggests our affections, emotions, and desires. Remember how the enemy darts penetrated first Eve's heart, stirring up unholy desires, and then Adam's. One of Solomon's wisest sayings was, 'Keep [i.e. guard] your heart with all vigilance; for from it flow the springs of life.'[15] Solomon would have been wiser still had he practised what he preached! He 'clung . . . in love' to many foreign women who turned away his heart from God and led him into idolatry.[16] He became a casualty through neglecting the breastplate.

The breastplate is righteousness, and Christ is our righteousness.[17] The moment we believed, the righteousness of Christ was paid into our heavenly account which was 'in the red' to the tune of thousands. Of course this radically altered our standing in heaven. But now we have to learn to use the cheque book of faith and live on these heavenly resources. This is practical righteousness. This means trusting Christ for grace to think right and act right, especially in our relationships with our fellow men.

The third piece of basic equipment is our *gospel sandals*. 'Having shod your feet with the equipment of the gospel of peace.' There is of course a place for aggressive witness, but the sandals, like the rest of the equipment, are to enable us to stand, not to march. The older versions have, 'the *preparation* of the gospel of peace', again something which is put on *before* the battle. What soldier would want to be caught by the enemy with his boots off?

The gospel sandals which enable the soldier to hold his ground refer, no doubt, to 'the defence and confirmation of the gospel'.[18] This will become increasingly important in the warfare of the end-time. Stephen was well shod when he made his great defence before the Council. Christ had warned His followers they would have to stand before rulers to bear witness. Writing to persecuted Christians Peter says, 'Be ready at all times to answer anyone who asks you to explain the hope you have in you.'[19] In other words, 'Be ready with your boots on.'

The Acts of the Apostles teaches us that to preach the gospel is to preach Christ. He is the gospel. A young friend asked my advice on how to handle some Jehovah Witnesses who were coming round for a talk. I said, 'Don't argue about doctrine, but preach Christ. Testify to what He has done for you.' Standing in these wonderful sandals we will never be moved from the faith of the gospel.

Now for the last three pieces, that we can seize and use in the moment of emergency. 'Above all taking *the shield of faith*.' 'Above all' because the shield is the large variety affording protection to the whole body, ideal for defensive warfare. When soldiers stand with these, shoulder to shoulder, they present an impenetrable wall. David often said that the Lord was his shield, but Paul says that faith is our shield. He becomes our shield as we exercise faith, but it must be faith in *Him*.

'With which you can quench all the flaming darts of the evil one.' If only our first parents had stood firm in their faith in God's love and wisdom, those flaming darts that ignited their unholy desires would have been put out at once. When later Christ was attacked with these they were immediately quenched, enabling Him to wield the sword with devastating effect. 'Do not throw away your confidence.'[20] Often the devil will use adverse circumstances to tempt us to abandon our shield. It was so with Peter when he denied His Lord. Jesus said, 'I have prayed for you that your *faith* may not fail.'

It is practically impossible to hold up one of these body shields and look down. To hold up the shield means to 'keep our eyes fixed on Jesus'.[21] Remember Peter walking on the water? When his eyes were on Jesus his faith was invincible. But when he looked at his circumstances the shield was lowered and swift came the darts of doubt and fear.

Increasingly is the mind of the believer becoming a battle-ground. Hence the importance of '*the helmet of salvation*'. We can say with David, 'The Lord is . . . my salvation.' He is the helmet. Salvation may be expressed in three tenses:

Past Tense: I have been saved from the *penalty* of sin.

Present Tense: I am being saved from the *power* of sin.

Future Tense: I will be saved from the *presence* of sin. The devil's attacks on the mind also come along these three lines. Even though our sins have been confessed and forgiven, he will try to attack us on our past record, and bring us into condemnation. Put on the helmet. 'There is no condemnation now for those who live in union with Christ Jesus . . . Who will accuse God's chosen people? God Himself declares them not guilty!'[22]

With others it is more the present relationships of life, the pressures and the problems that adversely affect their thought life. They are tempted to give way to bitter, jealous, proud or impure thoughts. There is complete deliverance and protection from all of these in the salvation of Christ.[23] As to the future, so many are haunted by fears of the unknown tomorrow, their health, their jobs, their finances, their families. The thought of nuclear war fills them with dread. They are afraid of death. What a need for the helmet of salvation. I *shall be* saved. Jesus is coming back to reign. My future is in His hands and He does all things well. Elsewhere Paul refers to the helmet as 'our hope of salvation'.[24] Only the Christian has justification for being an optimist. But more of this in the closing chapter.

Finally, we are to take '*the sword of the Spirit* which is the word of God'. Here again the sword is defensive, to enable us to stand. Some say that 'the sword' is the Bible, yet there are many Christians who hold the Bible in their hands and even store it in their minds, who have never used this sword. 'Word' here means *utterance*. 'The sword of the spirit which is the utterance that comes from God.' To wield the sword we must *speak* to Satan, and say in faith as Jesus did, 'It is written.' This will compel him to leave.

As with each other part of the soldier's equipment, the sword refers to Christ. He is 'the word of God'. There is great power in declaring His name, His character, His victory. You will find the scriptures in the appendix on 'Our Authority over Satan' will help. They are worth memorising. But remember it is the Spirit's sword. There is nothing magical in the words. But when the Spirit inspires them they will be effective.

In this armour God has made provision for our complete protection. Clad in it the enemy will not be able to touch us. He may make repeated attacks but he will never move us from our position of victory in Christ. And then, great will be our joy, 'having fought to the end, to remain victors on the field.'[25]

[1] Eph. 1. 3   [2] Eph. 6. 12   [3] Eph. 2. 4–6   [4] Eph. 1. 19–21   [5] Eph. 2. 6 RSV   [6] Eph. 6. 11, 13   [7] verse 10   [8] Rom. 13. 14 RSV   [9] Psa. 18. 2   [10] verses 11, 13   [11] *God's Freedom Fighters* by David C. K. Watson (p. 76)   [12] Heb. 12. 1   [13] 1 Cor. 6. 12 RSV   [14] John 8. 32, 36   [15] Prov. 4. 23   [16] 1 Kings 11. 1–4   [17] 1 Cor. 1. 30 RSV   [18] Phil. 1. 7 RSV   [19] 1 Pet. 3. 15   [20] Heb. 10. 35 RSV   [21] Heb. 12. 2   [22] Rom. 8. 1, 33   [23] Eph. 4. 22–24   [24] 1 Thess. 5. 8   [25] verse 13 Weymouth's Translation

15

ENTANGLEMENTS

A SOLDIER's life calls for great dedication. He cannot get deeply involved in outside interests and at the same time be an effective soldier. Paul puts it this way: 'A soldier in active service wants to please his commanding officer, and so does not get mixed up (entangled RSV) in the affairs of civilian life.'[1] The world in which we are called to serve Christ is full of entanglements. Many promising soldiers of Christ have become ineffective or have even deserted through the lure of the world. Paul recounted with great sadness, 'Demas fell in love with this present world and has deserted me.'[2]

In the parable of the Sower, Jesus warned us of some of these dangers. The thorns that choked the good seed He interpreted as being 'the worries about this life, the love for riches, and all other kinds of desires'.[3] In James's view, for one united to Christ to court the friendship of the world is to commit spiritual adultery.[4] According to John, to have in your heart the love of the world is to be devoid of the love of the Father.[5]

Let us look at these worries, riches, and desires of which Jesus spoke. Take note that worrying is a form of worldliness, for Jesus classed it with the love of money and worldly pleasure. The root of worrying is unbelief. Is not a soldier's food, clothing and every other necessity the responsibility of his commander? 'So do not start worrying: "Where will my food come from? or my drink? or my clothes?" (These are the things the heathen are always after.) Your Father in heaven knows that you need all these things.'

Then there is 'the love for riches' which Paul said was 'a source of all kinds of evil'.[7] Money is not evil in itself since we need it to live. It is when it gets into our hearts that the trouble begins. Men do not love money for itself, but for the power, influence and prestige that it brings, and the material things it will procure. Greed for money lies behind much political activity and most industrial unrest. It is a powerful weapon in the hands of Satan.

The man of the world looks upon earthly treasure as his security. But Jesus showed how insecure this was. Earthly treasure could be ruined—'moths and rust destroy'. It could be removed—'robbers break in and steal'. You could be taken from it—'You fool! This very night you will have to give up your life; then who will get all these things . . .?'[8] No wonder the Bible speaks of riches as 'an uncertain thing'.[9]

How are we to safeguard ourselves against this snare of the devil? First we are to resist the spirit of the age that is always greedy for more, and to cultivate a spirit of contentment. 'Keep your lives free from the love of money, and be satisfied with what you have.'[10] Then, we are to recognize that the money that God permits us to handle is a sacred trust. We are not to be mean, selfish, or extravagant. We are to give generously—to the work of God and the servants of God and the needy—as the Lord prospers and directs us. The Israelite gave a 'tithe' (tenth) of his income to God as a basic minimum. The New Testament Christian certainly should not give less. 'God loves the one who gives gladly.'[11]

Finally, instead of placing our 'hope' on riches, we are to place it 'on God, who generously gives us everything for us to enjoy'.[9] This is true security for He has promised to take care of all the needs of His children. What a privilege to trust such a rich and generous Heavenly Father.

The third entanglement Jesus mentioned was 'all other kinds of desires'. A great variety of things may come under this category. Like riches, many of them will not be sinful in themselves, but become an entanglement because of the place that is given to them in the heart and life. The thorns 'choked' the good seed. If a desire is arresting my spiritual growth then let me free myself from it, even if this means taking drastic action.

In Luke's account of this parable, these 'desires' are referred to as the 'pleasures of life'.[12] Though we live in a pleasure-mad world, we should not assume that 'pleasure' is necessarily a dirty word. Very many who make no profession of faith look upon Christianity as going to church on the one hand, and giving up all pleasures on the other. How boring!

In certain Christian circles worldliness has almost been reduced to a set of 'Thou shalt nots'. This living by a legal code is a snare into which the Pharisees fell. It led them to emphasise the wrong thing and to make a wrong judgment of others. They even accused our Lord of being a worldling. 'Look at this man!' they cried, 'He is a glutton and wine-drinker, and a friend of tax collectors and outcasts.'[13] It led to inconsistency, taking pride in the scrupulous observance of what was incidental, while neglecting the things that really mattered. Christ called them 'Blind guides!' adding, with a touch of ironic humour, 'You strain a fly out of your drink, but swallow a camel!'[14]

No, following Christ will never 'cramp our style'. Not only does God give all things generously for our enjoyment, but promises to withhold 'no good thing' if we walk uprightly.[15] It is the devil's lie, often sustained by the wrong attitude of believers, that Christianity is a 'kill-joy' affair, and 'goodbye' to a full and satisfying life. The very reverse is the truth. We have been called to a life of liberty, not restriction. The Lord denies us nothing, except that which would injure us, or maybe others.

Though the soldier of Christ is not to be entangled by the world, nor is he to be isolated from it. Separation to Christ and His cause does not mean seclusion. Christ told us to be 'salt', that is, to be His preservative in a decaying society. You cannot preserve fish by putting the fish in one barrel and the salt in another! Nor can we segregate ourselves, and at the same time permeate and preserve society. Jesus was rightly called 'the friend of sinners', and yet in His spirit and standard He was always a Man apart. He never compromised His convictions. We are called to be like Him.

There are no set rules in Scripture on these matters, only guiding principles. It is important that we apply these carefully, and so avoid being entangled. They will enable us to decide for ourselves many other doubtful matters. But God's word is very clear—we are not to judge others who decide differently.[16] Speaking of 'doubtful things' Paul says, 'Nothing is unclean of itself'.[17] What may be wrong for one may be right for another. What may be wrong for me in this set of circumstances may be right in that. These are the questions I need to ask:

Can I do this with a clear conscience and a heart at peace? 'Happy is the man who does not feel himself condemned when he does what he approves of!'[18]

Can I enter into it wholeheartedly? 'Whatever your hand finds to do, do it with your might.'[19]

Can I do this to the glory of God? 'Whatever you do, whether you eat or drink, do it all for God's glory.'[20]

Can I do this in Christ's name (i.e. as His representative)? 'Everything you do or say, then, should be done in the name of the Lord Jesus.'[21]

Can I kneel down and thank God for this thing? 'Everything you do or say, then, should be done . . . as you give thanks . . . to God the Father.'[21]

Will it be helpful to my spiritual life? ' "All things are lawful" but not all things are helpful. "All things are lawful" but not all things build up.'[22]

Will it enslave me? 'I could say, "I am allowed to do anything"; but I am not going to let anything make a slave of me.'[23]

Will it endanger my health? 'Don't you know that your body is the temple of the Holy Spirit, who lives in you . . . Use your bodies for God's glory.'[24]

Will it minister to my fallen nature or lead me into temptation? 'Stop giving attention to your sinful nature, to satisfy its desires.'[25]

Is it in keeping with a proper stewardship of time and money? 'Look carefully then how you walk, not as unwise men but as wise, making the most of the time.'[26] 'The man to whom much is given, of him much is required.'[27]

Will it stumble my brother who may be weaker than I? 'Be careful, however, and do not let your freedom of action make those who are weak in the faith fall into sin.'[28]

Is it likely to be misunderstood? 'So do not let what is good to you be spoken of as evil . . . Let us then pursue what makes for peace and for mutual up-building.'[29]

Of course no one will ask all these questions every time, but as you imbibe the principles your conviction of what is right or wrong for you will most often be instinctive.

Susannah Wesley in a letter to her son Charles, later to become the gifted hymn writer, summarises much of what has been said:

Whatever dulls the sensitiveness of my spirit towards God, or takes the fine edge off my thought of Him—must be ruled out, for *He is my Lord*.

Whatever injures or weakens my body, or affects the mastery of it—must be ruled out, for *it is the temple of the Lord*.

Whatever adversely affects the clearness of my witness to Jesus Christ before others—must be ruled out, for it was *His parting wish that I should be a witness of Him*.

Whatever may cause my brother to stumble in his Christian life—must be ruled out, for *that would grieve Jesus*.

As Christ's soldiers let us be dedicated to Him and avoid being entangled.

[1] 2 Tim. 2. 4   [2] 2 Tim. 4. 10   [3] Mark 4. 19   [4] Jam. 4. 4 AV   [5] 1 John 2. 15   [6] Mat. 6. 31–32   [7] 1 Tim. 6. 10   [8] Mat. 6. 19; Luke 12. 20   [9] 1 Tim. 6. 17   [10] Heb. 13. 5; 1 Tim. 6. 6–9   [11] 2 Cor. 9. 7   [12] Luke 8. 14   [13] Luke 11. 19   [14] Mat. 23. 23–24   [15] Psa. 84. 11   [16] Rom. 4. 1–4, 10–13   [17] Rom. 4. 14   [18] Rom. 14. 22; Acts 24. 16; Col. 3. 15   [19] Eccl. 9. 10; Col. 3. 23   [20] 1 Cor. 10. 31   [21] Col. 3. 17   [22] 1 Cor. 10. 23 RSV   [23] 1 Cor. 6. 12   [24] 2 Cor. 6. 19–20   [25] Rom. 13. 14; Gal. 5. 13   [26] Eph. 5. 15–16 RSV   [27] Luke 12. 48   [28] 1 Cor. 8. 9; Rom. 15. 1–2   [29] Rom. 14. 16, 19 RSV

16

DISCIPLINE

IF discipline is weak, even the best equipped army is liable to crack when faced with hardship or adversity. Of course discipline is an unpopular word in a society where authority is being attacked and undermined. Here the attitude of the Christian soldier must stand out in sharpest contrast to the spirit of the age. We are called to be disciples, that is, disciplined men. This is a vital element in Christian soldiering.

It is a tremendous truth that we 'do not live under law but under God's grace'.[1] This is setting many free from a life of struggling and bringing them into victory. Trying to live the Christian life by rules and regulations only leads to defeat and frustration. 'Christ has set us free!' exclaims Paul, 'Stand, then, as free men, and do not allow yourselves to become slaves again.'[2] But we must not forget that he goes on to say, 'Do not let this freedom become an excuse for letting your physical desires rule you'.[3] When liberty leads to licence you end up with a worse kind of slavery. It's great to step on the accelerator, but if you don't know how to apply the brake you're heading for trouble! Liberty must be balanced by discipline.

A child needs to be disciplined by parents and teachers. But this is only to help him to discipline himself and so be fitted for responsibility. How can he control others if he has never learned to control himself? So it is self-discipline, or 'self-control'[4] to use the Bible word, which I want to emphasise in this chapter. This means firstly facing up to the temptations of the body.

Our bodies are only evil in so far as they are dominated by our fallen nature. Through grace we are freed from this dominion.[5] Then the body becomes an instrument to serve the plan of God. It is like a telephone by which the world communicates with us, and we with the world. This is why we are told to present our bodies to God[6] that Christ may be expressed through us.

The Creator has placed within us bodily desires, for food, for sleep, and for sex. Through 'the fall' these appetites, given for our enjoyment as well as the necessary preservation of life, have got out of hand. Very often they master us when we should master them. A hearty appetite degenerates into gluttony, a healthy desire for sleep into laziness, and normal sex desire, which God designed for marriage, into lust and licentiousness. Self-discipline means gaining the mastery over our appetites just as a colt has to be broken in. Paul puts it this way: 'I could say, "I am allowed to do anything"; but I am not going to let anything make a slave of me.'[7]

The seeking of sensual pleasure only proves the

truth of Jesus' words, 'Whoever drinks this water will get thirsty again'. But dissatisfaction and frustration are not the most serious consequences of throwing self-restraint to the winds. The door of the human personality is thus opened to evil spirits. Drug-taking has the same effect. 'A man without self-control is like a city broken into and left without walls.'[8]

Where a nation makes sensual pleasure its goal, as did ancient Rome, it is sowing the seeds of its own destruction. It is here the Christian soldier must fight for Christian standards. He is to be salt in a decaying society. But what if the salt has lost its taste? What if the Christian himself is enslaved to his own appetites? How can he fight the corruption around him? Vigilance will always be needed, for even great men have lapsed badly here. Noah is described as a blameless man who walked with God, and yet his son found him in his tent drunk and naked.[9]

Self-discipline, however, is not simply a question of overcoming the sins of the flesh. It enables the Christian to win the prize in the spiritual contest. 'Every athlete in training submits to strict discipline;' explains Paul, 'he does so in order to be crowned with a wreath that will not last; but we do it for one that will last for ever.'[10] If the athlete does not exercise self-discipline that 'extra' he needs in the race will not be there, and someone else will breast the tape first. Similarly, the soldier will be unable to endure suffering, to hold out in the day of adversity, and will win no decoration for his part in the battle.

So the matter is one of great importance if we have an eye for the coming day of reckoning and reward.

The disciplining of the mind is no less important than that of the body. Our minds are under constant bombardment by enemy propaganda. How easily the thought life becomes infected by pride, uncleanness, ambition, or jealousy. We are afflicted with wandering thoughts or we waste time in foolish daydreaming. The New Testament makes it quite clear that we are responsible to discipline our minds.

Peter writes to believers facing end-time persecutions and pressures—a message which will become increasingly relevant as the age draws to its close. He has some important things to say about the mind.[11] 'Have your minds ready for action,' or as the older versions have it, 'Gird up the loins of your mind'—a fitting word for the scatter-brained! Later he says, 'The end of all things is near. You must be self-controlled and alert [keep sane and sober RSV], to be able to pray.' Both words suggest a disciplined state of mind, not intoxicated by the spirit of the age. Paul is even more explicit. He says, 'We take every thought captive and make it obey Christ.'[12]

Closely associated with the mind are the emotions and affections. These too must be disciplined. In his Patmos vision John sees the glorified Son of Man 'with a golden girdle round his breast',[13] that is, His affections and emotions are controlled by His divine character. Though at times Jesus displayed deep emotion He was never carried away by His feelings. If we find ourselves overcome by excitement, fear, anger or resentment we need to take our emotions in hand. Paul reminded Timothy, 'God did not give us a spirit of timidity but of power and love and self-control.'[14]

Perhaps it is the tongue that calls for the greatest self-control of all. What irreparable damage has been done to the cause of Christ by criticism, gossip, slander, back-biting, misrepresentation, exaggeration, and many other activities of that small unruly member. James, who has most to say about this, insists that a man's religion is worthless if he hasn't learned to control his tongue, but that the man who never slips up here is perfect, and is able to control his whole body.[15] 'No man has ever been able to tame the tongue,'[16] declares James, and yet the tongue *must* be tamed. What is impossible to man is possible to God.

How is all this self-discipline to be accomplished? First we must recognise that it is not only needed but commanded of us as soldiers of Christ, therefore it must be possible. To assert otherwise would be to make God a tyrant. Second we must admit that we cannot do it ourselves. It is not dependent on our strength of will, so we are all in the same boat here.

Thirdly, there must be within us a God-given determination to take ourselves in hand with the strength that He gives. Discipleship means saying 'No!' to self by embracing the cross.[17] So many of us pamper when we ought to pummel. Paul says, 'I harden my body with blows and bring it under complete control.'[18] And again, 'Endure hardness, as a good soldier of Jesus Christ.'[19] Augustine spoke of having toward God a heart of flame, toward man a heart of love, and toward himself *a heart of steel*.

Finally, we must reckon on the fact of the cross, and of the indwelling Spirit. Look again at the opening of Romans 6. Remember what happened to us when Jesus died. Move on to chapter 8 and read Paul's triumphant declaration: 'The law of the Spirit, which brings us life in union with Christ Jesus, has set me free from the law of sin and death.'[20] Remember, 'self-control' (literally, 'inward strength') is not the fruit of our striving but 'the fruit of the Spirit'.[21]

Fasting, a practice encouraged in the Bible, may greatly help us in this whole matter of self-discipline. This is fully dealt with in my book, GOD'S CHOSEN FAST (see back cover).

[1] Rom. 6. 14   [2] Gal. 5. 1   [3] ver. 13   [4] Gal. 5. 23 (temperance AV) [5] Rom. 8. 1–4   [6] Rom. 12. 1 RSV [7] 1 Cor. 6. 12   [8] Prov. 25. 28   [9] Gen. 6. 9; 9. 21   [10] 1 Cor. 9. 25   [11] 1 Pet. 1. 13; 4. 7; cf. 5. 8   [12] 2 Cor. 10. 5 [13] Rev. 1. 13 RSV   [14] 2 Tim. 1. 7 RSV   [15] Jam. 1. 26; 3. 2   [16] Jam. 3. 8   [17] Luke 9. 23 RSV   [18] 1 Cor. 9. 27 [19] 2 Tim. 2. 3 AV   [20] Rom. 8. 2   [21] Gal. 5. 22–23 RSV

17

MORALE

PSYCHOLOGICAL warfare is nothing new. The redskin practised it when he brandished his tomahawk and charged the foe with a blood-curdling yell! In every battle morale has always been of crucial importance. The finest and best equipped army becomes an easy prey once it is demoralised. Occasionally God Himself employed psychological warfare when He thundered against Israel's enemies before ever battle was joined. The devil too uses the psychological approach when he comes 'as a roaring lion', and we have already seen how we must be protected by 'the helmet of salvation'. I want now to show how to maintain a morale of the highest order, even in the midst of the fiercest battle.

The devil is a pastmaster at attacking the Christian soldier with doubt and fear, discouragement and depression. In addition to the protection afforded by our armour, we need to know how we may hit back and even seize the initiative. There are two weapons we must learn to use—joy and praise. They are the greatest morale-boosters I know, and the enemy finds them thoroughly demoralising.

Joy, like self-control, is part of 'the fruit of the

Spirit', and joy is one way in which the Spirit's power is expressed. If you are a joyful Christian you are a strong Christian, 'for the joy of the Lord is your strength'.[1] It was the radiant joy-filled lives of those early believers that took the Roman Empire by storm. Satan had no answer, and multitudes were drawn like a magnet to Christ.

It was not that these early Christians found their new life a bed of roses. Far from it. Deprivation, suffering, persecution, and even death were the order of the day. But this only caused their joy to stand out in sharper relief, and to prove that it was no superficial emotion. Christ's disciples had seen this same joy in the life of their Master. He had spoken of His joy being in them and had prayed to the Father that they would experience it fully.[2]

There is a paradox here. Jesus was 'a man of sorrows' and yet He knew this deep abiding joy. At the cross His cup of sorrow was full, yet even there 'because of the joy that was waiting for Him, He thought nothing of the disgrace of dying on the cross'.[3] It was the same with Paul. Called to endure the most intense suffering and hardship, he calmly declares, 'although saddened, we are always glad.'[4] And again, 'I am happy about my sufferings for you.'[5]

Let us visit the apostle in the prison at Rome. Shackled day and night to the soldier that guards him, he dictates a letter to the believers at Philippi. Not a word of complaint or self-pity, but a letter brim-full of joy. 'Rejoice in the Lord always,' quotes

Paul. The scribe lifts his quill from the parchment and looks up at the kindly face lined by years of suffering. 'Did you say "*always*", Paul?' 'Yes, always —and I'll say it again, Rejoice.' [6]

The Lord had told His disciples to 'dance for joy' [7] when they were persecuted for His sake. Such a command is quite ridiculous to those who only know a happiness that depends on happenings. Jesus never promised us blue skies and calm seas; in fact He warned of storms and tempests, [8] but promised that we would have His joy. It is strange but true that the persecuted Christians of Eastern Europe know much more about this 'great and glorious joy, which words cannot express' [9] than their brothers in the free West.

Paul names joy as one of the three characteristic features of the kingdom of God, [10] so we are not dealing here with a secondary matter. He often links it with peace, and shows us that it is the product of faith. [11] One thing is clear: we can never dissociate it from the ministry of the Holy Spirit. [12] Because He comes to make Christ real, fulness of the Spirit and fulness of joy go hand in hand. [13]

This joy of the Holy Spirit inevitably finds its outlet in expression of praise to God. Praise, according to the Psalmist, is joy's safety valve, [14] while James asks, 'Is anyone happy? He should sing praises.' [15] Thanksgiving and praise honour God, [16] and there is no higher service that we can render. It often releases the power of God to work in extraordinary ways. As soon as Jonah in the belly of the great fish raised 'the voice of thanksgiving', ascribing deliverance to the Lord, he *was* immediately delivered.[17] Paul and Silas in the inner dungeon, their backs bleeding and their feet fixed in the stocks, spent the midnight hour 'praying and singing hymns to God'.[18] The Lord responded with an earthquake which freed them from their fetters—and the jailer from his sins!

Perhaps the outstanding example of the power of praise as a weapon against the enemy is when Israel was invaded in the reign of Jehoshaphat. He called the nation to prayer and fasting, and God gave the assurance of victory. Next day they went into battle with a choir as their vanguard 'who were to sing to the Lord and praise Him in holy array'.[19] The moment the choir began to praise, God routed the enemy. Satan trembles when soldiers of Christ have 'the high praises of God . . . in their throats and two-edged swords in their hands'.[20]

Scripture often speaks of the *sacrifice* of praise or thanksgiving. This is a timely reminder that this weapon costs something to wield. People often say, 'But I just don't feel like praising.' I don't suppose Jonah felt like it. He probably felt a bit hot and clammy! I don't suppose Paul and Silas felt like it, with bleeding backs in a dark, dank, smelly dungeon. We are not invited to praise when we feel like it; we are commanded to praise continually,[21] to give thanks *for* everything and *in* everything.[22] This is what God wants, and this is the *sacrifice* that glorifies Him.

Like joy, praise is so very much the overflow of the Spirit-filled life. So many testify to a wonderful release in praise when the Lord Jesus baptised them in the Holy Spirit. The Ephesian believers had been filled, but Paul exhorts them, 'Go on being filled with the Spirit' (literal translation) and show it by singing 'hymns and psalms to the Lord, with praise in your hearts'.[23] Note that last phrase. It is so important that it is a heart matter and not simply a form of words. A 'praise patter' is obnoxious both to the ear of God and man. But when praise wells up from a heart that is inspired by the Holy Spirit it will both honour God and harass the devil. So train yourself to use the weapons of joy and praise.

[1] Neh. 8. 10   [2] John 15. 11; 17. 13   [3] Heb. 12. 2   [4] 2 Cor. 6. 10   [5] Col. 1. 24   [6] Based on Phil. 4. 4 RSV   [7] Luke 6. 23   [8] John 16. 2, 33   [9] 1 Pet. 1. 8   [10] Rom. 14. 17   [11] Rom. 15. 13   [12] Gal. 5. 22; 1 Thess. 1. 6 etc.   [13] Acts 13. 52   [14] Psa. 47. 1   [15] Jam. 5. 13   [16] Psa. 50. 23   [17] Jonah 2. 9–10   [18] Acts 16. 25   [19] 2 Chron. 20. 21–22   [20] Psa. 149. 6   [21] Heb. 13. 15   [22] Eph. 5. 20; 1 Thess. 5. 18   [23] Eph. 5. 18–19

18

THE FINAL BATTLE

In the opening chapter I spoke of the nature of this conflict that inevitably involves us all. It is the fight between light and darkness, between good and evil, between God and Satan. But how is the battle going? Anyone trying to assess this impartially might be excused for concluding that the devil was winning hands down! But the man who studies Bible prophecy is neither surprised nor dismayed. He knows that God never promised that the gospel would gradually christianise the world. He knows that God's present purpose is to call out of the world a people for Christ called the church.[1] He knows that while God is accomplishing this, often with powerful movements of His Spirit, the world situation will continue to worsen, with increasing tribulation, lawlessness and evil.[2]

How then will it all end? Imagine a game of chess, Right versus Wrong, in which Wrong seems to be sweeping the board. But Right is calmly waiting for that strategic moment when He will move One Piece, and say to Wrong, 'Checkmate!' Yes, it is God, not Satan, who will have the last move, and that will be the promised return of Jesus Christ to Planet

Earth. Not this time in humility and obscurity, but with myriads of angels as His escort, in the most dazzling display of power and splendour this world has ever seen.

Both Old and New Testaments abound with predictions of this great event. In fact there are many more prophecies concerning Christ's second coming than His first. It will be the vindication of God's whole plan of redemption, for it will involve the overthrow of Satan and all his hosts. The book of Revelation provides a fitting climax to the Bible, for this final battle and the events leading up to it are its central theme.

Though Christians are basically agreed on the fact of Christ's return, there are considerable differences in the interpretation of prophecy. Much of it is obscure or capable of more than one interpretation, especially the book of Revelation with its vivid symbolism. God could have made it all perfectly plain, so there is a wise reason why He has not done so. We are dealing with 'God's secret wisdom, hidden from men',[3] so no computer, whether mechanical or human, is capable of feeding us with the right answers. We are shut up to the teaching of the Holy Spirit that we may be preserved from human speculation. In this chapter I shall be dealing with basic facts rather than controversial details.

At the end of His earthly life Jesus spoke to His disciples of His departure to His Father's abode to prepare a home for them there. Then He added, 'And after I go and prepare a place for you, I will come back and take you to myself, so that you will be where I am.'[4] This promise was not fulfilled by His coming back to them in resurrection, nor by His coming in the person of the Holy Spirit, nor in the sense in which He came to them at death. What Jesus meant was made plain to them on the Mount of Olives.

In the act of blessing them Jesus was parted from them. They watched Him soar heavenwards till a cloud obscured Him from their sight. Still gazing upwards with the forlorn hope that perhaps He might reappear, they were startled by voices beside them. 'This Jesus,' said the two angels, 'who was taken up from you into heaven, will come back in the same way that you saw Him go to heaven.'[5]

'This Jesus'—not God the Father; not even Jesus in the person of the Holy Spirit—but Jesus Himself 'will come back'. That means His return will be *personal*. Then He would come back 'in the same way'. He had left them in a real body, for Thomas had been invited to put his hand into his Master's wounded side. So His return would be *physical*. Then in Revelation we read, 'Look! He is coming with the clouds! Everyone will see Him.'[6] That means His return will also be *visible*. There is a prophecy that suggests He will even return to earth at the very same spot, the Mount of Olives.[7]

God revealed to Paul that this great event in its first phase would involve the rapture (carrying away) of the saints. 'There will be the shout of command, the archangel's voice, the sound of God's trumpet, and the Lord Himself will come down from heaven! Those who have died believing in Christ will be raised to life first; then we who are living at that time will all be gathered up along with them in the clouds to meet the Lord in the air. And so we will always be with the Lord.'[8]

Concluding a great chapter on the resurrection of the body, Paul states: 'Listen to this secret: we shall not all die, but in an instant we shall all be changed, as quickly as the blinking of an eye, when the last trumpet sounds. For when it sounds, the dead will be raised immortal beings, and we shall all be changed.'[9] This change, of course, refers to our resurrection bodies rather than a moral or spiritual transformation. It is in this sense that we shall then be made like Christ.[10] The change will be instantaneous and permanent, and will fit us for a new mode of existence where we shall dwell in the presence of the Lord for ever.

What will this second coming of Christ mean for the world? For those who have rejected Him it will mean judgment. In His parables Jesus often taught that His coming at the end of the age would mean the punishment and destruction of the ungodly.[11] Paul referred to the coming of the Lord as being with flaming fire to punish the godless and unrepentant with 'eternal destruction.'[12] This solemn prospect should sober us up and send us out to reach others while grace still holds the door open.

What will Christ's coming mean to the careless or disloyal soldier of Christ? Jesus warned His disciples repeatedly that His coming would be sudden and unexpected, like a thief in the night.[13] For this reason they were to be watchful and prayerful, and not be caught unawares like the rest of mankind.[14] The command to watch is now more necessary than ever for the temptation to fall asleep is that much greater just before the dawn. Some believers will evidently be found unprepared for this sudden meeting with the Lord, else why the oft-repeated warnings?

Both the gospels and the epistles teach that when Christ returns He will judge the character and conduct of His servants, and deal with them accordingly.[15] The soldier who has been disloyal, guilty of misconduct, or who is found unprepared can only expect rebuke from his Commander, loss of privilege, and to have his wrong-doing exposed and dealt with.[16] This is why John urges us to abide in Christ 'so that we may be full of courage when He appears and need not hide in shame from Him on the Day He comes'.[17] No wonder John speaks of this great event as a purifying hope.[18]

What will that day mean to the loyal soldier of Christ, with no back-log of unconfessed sin, who has kept alert and prayerful, waiting for His Commander to appear? He will be able to look His Master in the face, see His smile of approval, and hear Him say, 'Well done, good and faithful servant.'[19] All the travail and tears, the sorrow and suffering that he was called upon to bear will then seem as nothing for the supreme joy of that moment. Best of all will be to enjoy the presence of his Master for ever, a joint-heir of His throne and His glory.[20]

Finally, what will that day mean for the great Commander Himself? Already He has waited almost two thousand years for His enemies to be made His footstool.[21] This then will be the hour of fulfilment, when the victory won on the cross will be vindicated before the whole universe.[22] This will be His coronation day, for not only shall every eye see Him, but 'all beings in heaven, and on earth, and in the world below will fall on their knees, and all will openly proclaim that Jesus Christ is the Lord'.[23] Perhaps His greatest joy will be to see in His glorified saints 'the fruit of the travail of His soul and be satisfied'.[24]

The story is told of a mother and daughter who steadfastly refused to yield to the Roman Emperor the allegiance due to Christ. Romans throng the Colosseum as they are led out to die. For one moment there is a hush as the two stand alone in the centre of the arena. Suddenly from high up in the gallery a voice rings out, vibrant and strong, across the great amphitheatre: 'Maranatha!'[25] ('Our Lord come' in Aramaic, the watchword of the early church). The lords and ladies turn to see whence comes this barbaric cry. Matron and maid lift their heads and a smile from another world lights up their faces. Then with a roar the lions are upon them, and two most

118

valiant soldiers have fought their last fight.

This hope that sustained saints and martyrs in their darkest hour will do so to the end of time. Men may take away from the Christian his position, his property, and even his very life, but they cannot rob him of his hope—that Christ will surely come, that his fidelity will be rewarded and his faith vindicated, that the end will be certain victory. As Peter would say, this is no 'cunningly devised fable', but sure and sober truth. Let it fill your vision, fortify your faith, purify your heart, and steel you for the fight. And then, having fought to the end, you too will stand with Christ at last, victor on the field of battle.

[1] Acts 15. 14; 1 Pet. 2. 9   [2] Mat. 24. 4–12; 2 Tim. 3. 1–5, 12–13; 4. 3–4 etc.   [3] 1 Cor. 2. 7   [4] John 14. 3   [5] Acts 1. 11   [6] Rev. 1. 7   [7] Zech. 14. 4   [8] 1 Thess. 4. 16–17   [9] 1 Cor. 15. 51–52   [10] Phil. 3. 20–21; 1 John 3. 2   [11] Mat. 13. 40–42, 49–50; 25. 41–46   [12] 2 Thess. 1. 6–9   [13] Luke 12. 39–40; cf. 1 Thess. 5. 2   [14] Luke 21. 34–36   [15] Mat. 25. 19; Luke 19. 15; Rom. 14. 10–12; 2 Cor. 5. 10   [16] Luke 19. 22; 1 Cor. 3. 12–15; 1 Cor. 4. 5; Col. 3. 25   [17] 1 John 2. 28   [18] 1 John 3. 3   [19] Mat. 25. 21   [20] Rom. 8. 17 RSV   [21] Heb. 10. 12–13   [22] Isa. 53. 12   [23] Phil. 2. 10, 11   [24] Isa. 53. 11   [25] 1 Cor. 16. 22

OUR AUTHORITY OVER SATAN

IF you memorise the following Scriptures they will become weapons in your armoury. These are taken from *Good News for Modern Man*. (*Today's English Version*), but you memorise them in the version which you generally use.

Eph. 6. 11, 17	Put on all the armour that God gives you, so that you will stand up against the devil's evil tricks. And accept . . . the word of God as the sword that the Spirit gives you.
Luke 10. 18–19	I saw Satan fall like lightning from heaven. Listen! I have given you authority . . . over all the power of the Enemy, and nothing will hurt you.
Jam. 4. 7	Submit yourselves to God. Resist the devil, and he will run away from you.
Col. 2. 15	And on that cross Christ freed Himself from the power of the spiritual

	rulers and authorities; He made a public spectacle of them by leading them as captives in His victory procession.
1 John 3. 8	The Son of God appeared for this very reason, to destroy the devil's works.
Heb. 2. 14–15	That through His death He might destroy the devil, who has the power over death, and so set free those who were slaves all their lives because of their fear of death.
1 John 4. 4	The Spirit who is in you is more powerful than the spirit in those who belong to the world.
Rev. 12. 11	Our brothers won the victory over him (Satan) by the blood of the Lamb, and by the truth which they proclaimed.
Mat. 12. 29	No one can break into a strong man's house and take away his belongings unless he ties up the strong man first; then he can plunder his house.
Mat. 18. 18–19	What you prohibit on earth will be prohibited in heaven; what you permit on earth will be permitted in heaven. . . . whenever two of you on earth agree about anything

you pray for, it will be done for you by My Father in heaven.

1 Cor. 15. 57 But thanks be to God who gives us the victory through our Lord Jesus Christ!